MW01292126

This book is a gift of in. wonderful smile tell you everything you need to know. Her story is genuine and real ... so you'll tear up. Her story is courageous and ultimately miraculous ... so you'll cheer. Be inspired! Then give this book away to inspire others!

—DAVID SANFORD, author of the forthcoming book, *Loving Your Neighbor* (Kregel, 2017)

Jeri was diagnosed with multiple myeloma, the same dreadful illness to which her mother had succumbed years ago. In her journey she courageously took on the physical, emotional, and spiritual challenges in her unique and positive way. Her story is an inspiration for us all, and particularly for anyone facing a discouraging diagnosis.

—DOUGLAS M. LACKOWSKI, MD, Kaiser Permanente Oncology.

In *Jeri Houle: My Story,* Jeri shares her life-threatening journey through cancer. However, even during difficult and scary times, she experiences the miraculous presence of Father God who infuses her with His love, turning the story of pain and suffering into one of thanksgiving and hope. Truly inspiring.

—JOAN B. WELLER, author of *The Journey of Intense Quietness.*

Jeri is all about finding meaning in her experience. She was always open to what God would reveal to her through her suffering, although I doubt she would call it suffering. Jeri continued to love Jesus and her faith seemed strengthened as she was amazed by His faithfulness, in even little details of life. She often shared the great and the small wonderful things God was working in her life, encouraging our staff and other patients. She is an inspiration to me.

—BELYNDA A. WOMACK, BA, RN, OCN, Kaiser Permanente.

"This book takes you through the highs and lows of walking thru the valley with cancer while holding on to Jesus' Hand thru it all and emerging victorious. Prepare to be inspired with Jeri's journey through uncharted territory. Find hope renewed. Experience faith abounding. Nothing will stop this diamond girl from shining!"

CINDY NOSACK, Personal friend
and traveling companion

"You have no idea what you are capable of."

BETTIE MITCHELL, founder of Good Samaritan Ministries
and author of *Whose Your Neighbor?*
and *Something Worth Saving*

Jeri Houle
My Story

of Courage and Hope
Fighting Blood Cancer

For Debbie,
Keep Shining my
Diamond Friend!
Jeri Houle

DEDICATION

To God - all for Your Glory! We made it through!!! You're not surprised! You were there the whole way. This is all about You! It's His-Story! I love You!

To KBH. Thank you for being on the path beside me, in sickness and in health, livin' life! I know you've got my back. I've got yours. Thanks for being patient as we learn each other's language. You challenge me to express how I'm really feeling instead of banging the pans. Your reminders that I haven't done anything WRONG, help a ton. Your laughter is good medicine. I love you!

To RWH and KEH. Let's keep choosing life and blessings. You've made me rich! Thanks for using your words to build! You are amazing young people and I am sooo proud of you. You've each had your own set of adversity. Thanks for showing me how strong you can be. I love you both!

In Loving Memory:
To Grandpa, who often said, "penny for your thoughts," wanting to know what I was thinking. I didn't always have the words, but I found the hidden message on the pennies that you gave me for trying, "In God We Trust." Thanks for listening with your heart and teaching me to trust. I love you!

In Loving Memory:
To Mom. Thank you for paving the way in life and through the uncharted medical journey. Your courage and positive outlook added a special quality to your years and to mine. I'm forever grateful. I love you!

CONTENTS

ACKNOWLEDGMENTS

To my Lord, Jesus Christ, the Giver of life, hope, and the surprise gift of writing.

My Stomping Team, family and friends, who received the emails in *real time* and sent back prayers, encouragement, texts, cards, messages, meals, quilts and thoughts that were spoken and unspoken. I've been carried.

To *CN* who helped me push through and to jump when all I wanted to do was freeze. One hundred days of pictures seems so long ago. We put lots of extra miles on your car and sharpened our swords. Bunny ears still make me laugh.

To *JW, BM, TD, JH, JH, JP, DH, NT* for all the extra time you spent on me, pouring out encouragement and rearranging your days to meet with me and help me adjust.

To Cancer Fighters and "Pit Dwellers" everywhere. There is always HOPE to hang on to and treasure to find in the midst of the storms. You never walk alone. It's a choice.

To Caregivers and Encouragers. Those who stay close day in and day out and answer the questions, "How is she/he doing?" Please know that you are in Good Hands, too. And Jesus will give you what you need to stay in the journey. Take good care of you, too!

To my medical community: doctors, nurses, schedulers, receptionists, phlebotomists, lab techs, housekeeping, nutrition services, curriers, and sanitation – you're all part of the team. Thank you!

To my book team: *DS, AA, KH, JG, CN, JW, BM, KJ* for answering all my questions, coaching me through the uncharted land of publishing, investing in me and putting the polish on the finished product.

WELCOME

I've been on a journey with God through the ups and downs of being diagnosed and treated for Multiple Myeloma, a blood cancer. Early on, in the midst of facing puzzling doctor visits, various invasive tests, gut wrenching waiting periods, and life and death issues, I found a verse in the Bible that brought me a lot of hope.

> ...Satan has demanded permission and tried his best to sift and separate you from me, like wheat. <u>But I (Jesus) have prayed for you</u> that your faith will not fail. You will not give in or give out. And you, once you have come through this time of testing, turn back again and strengthen your brothers (LUKE 22:31-32 NASB/ MSG/NIV – my combination).

I went through the "sifting"; it was a battle. The anticipated and feared chemotherapy, mild side effects, physical, emotional and mental fatigue started right away. Then came the frustrating restrictions, three weeks of hospitalization, and a Stem Cell Transplant which included multiple blood transfusions, countless lab work-ups, total hair loss, weakness, muscle atrophy. The nausea, vomiting, and diarrhea lasted for weeks. Napping, fragmented thoughts and actions, sorting out emotions, facing fears, shifts in priorities, reevaluating what really matters were all just part of my new normal: a shift to HOPE!

It was a big test!

But I would NOT change the path of this journey knowing the strength and inner healing I am experiencing on the other side of the battle.

During this medical process, writing became a significant outlet for me. I was inspired. I sent out email updates to family and friends. I had amazing support. There were a number of people who suggested writing a book, saying they were inspired in their own life journey by reading the way I was handling mine. This confirmed what I felt Jesus was telling me. I just didn't know that I could really do it and writing a book was the last thing on my mind at the time. But, I kept writing. And, as I re-read the words I had been inspired to put down on paper, the stories impacted me all over again.

As my health improved and my thinking cleared, I got serious about putting this project together. So, you are holding a collection of some of the stories, insights, and emails that were written during the first two years of the battle. You may be in your own battle. Press on. You're not alone. Hopefully you will also find some strength and encouragement for your own journey as you read through my *His-story.*

There is Hope.

I invite you to come along as I recount bits and pieces. The stories I call *Snapshots,* because at one point these stories lay on the table much like a collection of photographs ready to be organized into a photo album. They are snippets of a moment in time. Now they are in a "book album." Hidden throughout the pages, you will find insights into things I discovered along the way. Think of it as a treasure hunt. Along with the insightful Snapshots, you will also find real-time emails that were sent out to inform family and friends of my journey. Sometimes in the email there will be a discovery that was first uncovered in a Snapshot. So it might sound like I am repeating myself. And I am. But it was in this recounting that I was encouraged. Hopefully, you will be too.

Other things in these pages include various word pictures, photographs, and doodles. Mid-way through is a *Full Circle* of family life that takes members of my family through the Gates of Heaven. The hidden gem, *Diamond Girl Story*, has been repeated many times, and continues to be my favorite. And towards the end there is an observation of how God has used this journey to put many broken pieces of my inside-life back together.

In writing down some of the details of this journey and getting them into print, my prayer is that the True Author, God, may use me as His "quill-pen" to write *His-story* and this project of hope would bring strength to my brothers and sisters. It's my assignment. My goal. I will not always be around to speak face to face, but I know *His-story* can repeat *itSelf* wherever hope needs to be shared.

There is HOPE.

"But dreary as that path must look to those who view it only from afar, it has tender lights and restful shades that no other walk in life can give."
(Russell)

I believe that there is an Almighty God who loves me. He is my heavenly Father. My Father sent His Son, Jesus Christ, to earth to pay for all my mistakes, to forgive me of my sins and the sins of the whole world. Once Jesus died, rose again and ascended into heaven, He sent the Holy Spirit. The Holy Spirit remains on earth to lead, to guide, and to comfort.

God works in mysterious ways. I don't begin to understand it all. But it's enough to know He's on my side.

There is also an enemy, the devil. He is also referred to as Satan. He is not on my side. Satan's plan is to kill, steal and destroy. There is a battle. However, Satan cannot win. God always has the victory and is always mighty. There really is a battle going on. Sometimes I am aware of it and other times it is an invisible battle.

God is here!

God can and does intercept the enemy's plans. He's given me authority, through Jesus, to trample on Satan and his plans.

There is HOPE!

I can't wait to see what God's gonna do with the victory He has given to me to rise up and live life after being given a death sentence of blood cancer, aka Multiple Myeloma.

I am living out this directive that I found when this battle first started…

> **"When you have gone through the time of testing, turn back and strengthen (encourage) your brothers"** (LUKE 22:31-32 NASB/MSG).

I will include family, sisters, friends, companions, anyone within the sound of my "voice."

My brother said to me,

"You have personified God."

Yes I have; He's very real to me. Jesus is my invisible Friend that will never leave. He may be quiet at times. That's okay. He's here!

> **Now may the God of hope fill you with all joy and peace as you trust in Him, so that you will overflow with hope by the power of the Holy Spirit** (ROMANS 15:13 NIV).

Come along!

God Wrapped
His Arms Around Us!

What a Gift! What a Guy!
GRAND!!

Major Rapids!
Hold On TIGHT!!
Suck Rubber!!!

OOOOOH!
That Was
COLD!

Stomping Team Unites!

The Dolls

SECTION 1: SUMMER 2012

Celebration... What?

Journey Begins:

Hold On Tight

This journey actually started a few years ago with a quietly whispered prayer, *"Whatever it takes, Lord, whatever it takes."* Whatever it takes to get my tired, battle-weary, grief-stricken life, and the health of my marriage in line. I had recently stepped away from a job I loved, to rest and to concentrate on our family. The hours I had worked were opposite of my husband. Our schedules and routines had been out of sorts. We had hardly seen each other and when we did we were tired and emotionally distant. Our marriage had hit some major *white water rapids. Whatever it takes.*

Along with my own inner circle of turbulence, as a couple, we were also adjusting to a number of family members dying and being promoted to heaven. Our kids were growing up, graduating from high school and moving on. Our daughter was planning to move out of state and our son had three major (aka: scary) surgeries...

"HOLD ON!!!"

As things were finally turning around for us as a couple, we attended a spring marriage conference at the Oregon Coast. We were asked to grade our self and our spouse on how we were doing. We both apologized for our shortcomings, asked for forgiveness, and talked about how to improve.

"He's a good man with a good heart
and he loves me." (Eggerich)

"Treat your wife like a queen. Live life now while you still
feel good. And don't wait until you retire to go places
and do the things you want to do."

We both had areas to polish but came away encouraged to work on living life TOGETHER! God wrapped His arms around us.

And so the journey continued.

I had said for years that I was going to the Grand Canyon when I turned fifty. I didn't know how it would happen, but that was my plan and the Big 5 0 July birthday was coming quickly! Even so, it was a surprise to me when my husband said he'd been on an Internet search and found a float trip on the Colorado River that ran right through 198 river miles of the Grand Canyon. I really had been on his radar!

With a grin, he asked, "Wanna go?"

With *happy tears* streaming down my face, I nodded. The trip was booked!!!

It would launch ON MY BIRTHDAY!!! What a gift. What a guy! Thank you, Jesus!

Prior to the float trip, on various dates and outings, we gathered supplies for our 20-lb river bags. We had been given a checklist and worked together to make sure we were both set! What an amazing turnaround on lots of levels. A time of *jubilee*!

With our bags completely packed, we loaded the plane and headed to the Canyon. Besides the breathtaking beauty and inspiring surroundings that helped name this Canyon, Grand, we had some vital instruction before loading our river pontoon- rafts:

Wear your life jackets at all times

Drink LOTS of water–repeat

In the major rapids:

Hold on tight–with BOTH hands

"Suck Rubber!"

(Meaning, lean forward so the water goes over your head rather than hitting you in the face.)

Little did we know that these instructions would soon be life lessons needed for day-to-day survival. But for the mean time these instructions kept us safe in one of THE most marvelous, amazing places on earth.

The River-to-Life analogies were spot on. We hit major rapids. We held on for all we were worth. We got slapped in the face with the reality of very cold water.

When we kept our eyes open, we saw the treasures. We met amazing people, frolicked in the waterfalls, splashed in the pools, enjoyed the food, got warmed to the core by the sun, slept under the stars/moon, hiked up major cliffs and hiked back down again. We laughed! Lived life! Enjoyed each other! What a way to start my 50th year!

As the helicopter took us from the canyon back to civilization and river-baths were replaced with hot showers, we didn't realize what was around the next bend...we went happily floating along.

"Can ya jump?"

Something Is Wrong

Soon after the Grand Trip, we spent an afternoon/evening with some classmates of mine and decided we would continue to get together. We were all turning 50 and reunions are much more fun with a potluck and laughter. We all knew in the back of our minds that hospitals and funerals linger in the sidelines of our futures. Enjoy it all while you can.

I also spent some time at my grandparent's farm clearing out a lifetime of belongings and getting to know a bit more of my paternal family history. With both my grandparents and now my dad joining other members of my extended family in heaven, it was a bittersweet time of discovery and closure.

As I settled back at home with a few more mementos than I needed, I noticed that my back was hurting. Stretching didn't help, neither did the Motrin. Hmmm...

Pulled muscle?

Strain?

Something strange...

I'd seen how miserable my husband had been with, what turned out to be kidney stones. I decided to have my situation checked out. My doctor's response after the quick exam...

"Probably strained muscles, but do a urine sample before you leave and stop by the lab for some blood work."

I was thinking, "She's going to tell me I definitely have kidney stones."

Before the end of the day, she called me at home....

"You have acute kidney failure. If you have any trouble in the night, go to ER. And see the doc at Urgent Care in the morning. I've ordered more tests!!!"

Major Rapids...Hold on TIGHT...Suck Rubber!!!!!!!!

And then there were more tests. Not knowing for sure what was really going on in my physical body, I knew emotionally and spiritually the river was getting "poppy" and the cold splash of reality was startling. Needing to find out WHY my kidneys weren't functioning properly was a puzzling time. And finally after even more tests, the diagnosis: Multiple Myeloma (MM), *a blood cancer*, with no known cure. I will explain more later.

When I was finally given a diagnosis, it was a relief, because the testing, trials, exploration, and waiting were finally over. I knew what was wrong. But then I KNEW what I was dealing with and it rocked my world. Cancer...ugh! It felt like someone had just punched me in the gut! Ugh!

Cancer. CANCER!!! CANCER!!!!!! The worst news ever!!!!

What did I do wrong?

Maybe I can eat different or add some special exercise.

They want to use Chemotherapy – the dreaded poison!

I don't want to put all that **** in my body.

Maybe I won't do anything.

I don't want to get sick.

Am I gonna die?

Really?!

I don't like this at all!!!

Lord, HELP!!!

My life was spinning out of control. This diagnosis ROCKED my world. There was a major battle inside. It went something like this:

God, I don't want to go through this. I'm really scared.

I don't know what's going on.

I've taken really good care of myself. IT'S JUST NOT FAIR!

NO! NO! NO!

Can I just skip this part? I'll come *home!*

Can I just come *home* to heaven with You now?

I just want to die.

I don't want to go through all this. I watched Mom in a puzzling battle with Multiple Myeloma. It's not fun!

Take me Home.

<Tears>

<Deep breath>

I wrestled.

I waited.

Can anything good come out of this?

Are You there, God?

Can You hear me?

Did You leave?

Is this the end?

Can I see You?

<Tears>

<Deep breath>

I wrestled.

I waited some more.

God, can You get glory out of this?

I'll go down this road if You say so.

I will fight to live and not give up.

But only if You get glory! If not, cancel the plans of the enemy and take me home.

God, I'll go through this **If** You go with me.

God, I'll go through this if You want me to...if You get the glory.

I'll get the glory if you share the story!

Show me how!

God, not my will but Yours.

Will You heal me?

I believe You can heal me. Help me with my unbelief.

I love you.

I am here with you.

I won't leave you.

It's not about you. I have a plan.

It's going to be okay!

I went searching the Bible for some answers and secured my Lifejacket. Verses of scripture flooded in, but the battle raged on.

"...I came that they might have life and might have it abundantly" (John 10:10 NASB).

Really? How does that work...more abundantly? Looks like mine is draining away!

I felt like I was drowning in the fear and future "what-ifs." Worry and doubt hit me again like that cold river water on the float trip.

HELP!

I've been trained to make choices in the trials, find the good in things so I can put on a happy face, and press on. So, with the cold chill of reality, I turned to another verse.

Bless the Lord, O my soul and ALL that is within me...

Everything inside of me must bow down to the name of Jesus. If it can't bow, it must leave...it's trespassing in my body.

Bless the Lord O my soul and forget none of His benefits,

Who pardons ALL your iniquities...

Remember all those things I've been forgiven for? Stop and think about it! He's done soooo much. Be thankful!!! It's a choice.

Who heals all your diseases?

Who redeems your life from the pit?

The Grand Canyon was a deep pit. So deep that at one point only a ribbon of sky remained. Eventually I got out. There is Hope.

Who crowns you with loving kindness and compassion?

Who satisfies your years with good things?

So that your youth is renewed like the eagle (Psalms 103:1-5 NASB – emphasis mine).

The eagle molts…do I have to molt?

Eventually, with my attitude adjusted, at least for the moment, word pictures came into my head. I started to doodle on paper. Peace replaced the tears; hugs settled some of the turmoil.

Hold on tight!!!

Let me stop for a moment and explain a few things. As a family, we made a deal years ago when my mom was going through her battle with cancer that we would be open, honest, and share what was really going on with her health issues…good or bad.

No secrets!

No surprises!

It was hard, but it worked for us.

It was the pattern we would continue throughout my own health battle. I began sending out emails. Writing became an outlet, a source of processing for me. It was a way of communicating to many without the fatigue of repeating myself. Writing created a major support system, of sorts. Also, I felt it was an assignment from God, a way for *His-story* to be shared.

So, I wrote to family. I went out on a limb and included those dear classmates I'd just seen earlier in the summer and some other dear friends. Not sure where this was going, but I felt opportunities for the miraculous need to be shared! Celebrated! I needed to reach out, even if I have to go through rough waters before the celebrations,. Besides, I didn't want to go it alone.

Here, Reader, we must back up a bit and allow the email communication to introduce my family and friends to this *Battle Project.*

Sent: Tuesday, August 28, 2012
Subject: Celebration...soon - Tough things first

Hi friends,

Celebrating is always a fun thing (just like this summer at our mini reunion-what a blast!!!) However, sometimes there are things that go on in our lives BEFORE we can celebrate that are a challenge. We don't like to talk about these things during the tough part for one reason or another. (We might look weak or embarrassed. It's nobody's business, don't want to bother anyone, just a little thing, etc. You're talking to the master of excuses. I've used them all.)

I'm discovering more and more that tough things are very much a part of life so... I'm going out on a limb a bit here and sharing a tough thing so in the future we can celebrate how it turns out!

This past week was spent in and out of doctor's offices, labs/tests for what they are calling, at least right now, "acute kidney failure." I have more tests this week and an appointment with a kidney specialist on Thursday. Let's just say, "There is a battle going on." I'm a strong fighter.

With all of that said, I need your thoughts and prayers.

I will keep you posted.

And remember - no matter the outcome, there is a celebration...soon!!!

In Good Hands,
Jeri

✇ Sent: Thursday, August 30, 2012
✇ Subject: Re: Celebration...soon - Doc Puzzled

Okay -

I promised to let you know what I found out today...not much.

These doctors are as puzzled as the others. They said that, other than my blood work and back pain, everything looks good.

More tests next week.

I did ask about all the water I drank in the Grand Canyon. The doctors didn't think that could be it.

In the mean time, I am to keep hydrated.

My Real Physician is in charge.

Jeri

✇ Sent: Thursday, September 6, 2012
✇ Subject: Re: Celebration...soon - Puzzle Saga

Hello again,

The kidney puzzle saga continues as the doctors try to figure things out.

Blood tests are still showing something *abnormal*. X-ray, ultra sound, and CT scan are NOT picking up anything. Needle biopsy is now scheduled for next Friday and yes more blood work.

Feeling pretty good besides a low backache and a bit tired.

Trusting in THE Physician,
Jeri

📧 Sent: Tuesday, September 11, 2012
📧 Subject: Re: Celebration...soon - Left Field Blood Tests

It's me.
Please let me know if you'd like me to take you off this continuing story.

Blood tests today... As the Kidney specialist said, "We're going out into left field." Which means they did tests that were very random. Trying to eliminate any "common issues that are presenting themselves in very uncommon ways."

It feels like I'm falling apart, like the way the eagle molts. But after a season the bird is renewed. Maybe this is my season of molting.
There is HOPE!

At Peace!!!
Thanks for praying.

They are checking for metals from environmental issues, including the Grand Canyon and the recent well-water drinking I did at the *family farm*.
Prayer is always good.
Thanks for checking in.

In Good Good Hands,
Jeri

Sent: Saturday, September 15, 2012
Subject: Re: Celebration...soon-Flank

The kidney biopsy, on Friday, went as they planned and my overnight observation stay in the hospital was uneventful in the eyes of the health-care-world. That's a good thing.

While I have never been tackled in the *flank* with a football helmet, I have a much-increased appreciation for what players endure *after-the-game*. A kidney biopsy hurts.

I am home now, in the quiet, and *non-vital-taking* comfort of my own space. No nurses interrupting my sleep. Home Sweet Home!!! Sleep Sweet Sleep!!!

Upcoming week:
Monday: Preliminary report from biopsy
Thursday: GYN consultation for growth in uterus-plan?
Friday: Kidney Specialist-final report from biopsy-answers?

The doctors are still puzzled and trying to name what is going on. I figure as they name *it, it* will become the specific prayer target.

I believe Jesus can heal, does heal, and has healed. My prayer is "Jesus, help me in my unbelief".

Still in Good Hands,

Jeri

Thanks for listening!!

📧 Sent: Monday, September 17, 2012
📧 Subject: Celebration…soon - Dark Clouds

Monday night,

No news from the doctors to report.

I'm happy to report the *dark cloud of doubt* that hovered over me this morning has cleared a bit…but waiting, wondering, anticipating is a battle!

I'll let you know when I hear something.

Jeri

Days of Discovery

On the float trip we had river guides who led the way, pointed out interesting landmarks, maneuvered through wild waterways, and told amazing stories within the deep canyon. We discovered that the Grand Canyon had been the last territory to be mapped in the United States, leaving it uncharted while much of the rest of the country was thriving. And while it's still declared a National Park, it is definitely a wilderness area. Beautiful in its own way, but unfamiliar. During our adventure, there were spots along the river where we all got out of the rafts and hiked along on trails. Sometimes we'd hike to a hidden waterfall, or along creek beds, or to viewpoints, or along a narrow cliff. To us, the path was unknown. We followed the guide.

With the medical journey, the path also seemed uncharted. But I had walked with the Lord long enough to know that I would never walk alone. He would guide me. He would point out some very interesting things. He stayed with me, even if I forgot He was there. I wasn't expecting the wild ride into the deep, dark, lonely pits. However the stories I was told there were amazing. As I found my footing on the Rock, the discoveries came pouring in to me as word pictures. There was the Fiery Furnace, The Diamond Girl, and the Feathered Hideout to start with, along with the action of Stomping. Later on stories relating to Storms, Fog, Rainbows, and Clearing Skies all helped to move me along in the *Uncharted Territory*.

Uncharted Territory and The Pit

This journey took me through *uncharted territory*. I went places, saw and experienced things that had never crossed my *path* before.

There was an actual path in the unmapped, unpredictable, uncharted territory. Whether it was chipped with bark, paved, graveled, carpeted, cemented, or tiled, there was a path. And it took me into strange, different, scary, and wonderful places, sometimes all in the same day. If someone were watching, they could see the action: doctors visits, rose gardens, walks, opera performance, dinners, beaches, labs, hospitals, candy shops, light displays, zoos, airports, libraries, Bible studies, waterfalls...

However, there was another path, a secret path that was not so obvious. This path was and is still hidden from the eye and the feet. This secret path leads me on a journey into the inside, into the heart and mind.

When the diagnosis of Multiple Myeloma (MM), a blood cancer, was being deliberated, my secret path was leading me to a deep, dark, slimy pit of emotions. I battled with fear, terror, anger, confusion, resentment, *why-me*, self-pity. Obsessive thoughts pulled me deeper into a pit of despair. I fell in. Stifling fear, crippling worry, and agonizing *what-ifs* all trying to push my head under, literally taking my life and breath away. I didn't want to do anything. I didn't want to go anywhere. I slept a lot. I wanted to wake up and have it all be over and go back to *normal*.

I was sinking!

I cried!

I'm gonna die.

I know we all die at some point, but it seems too early.

I just turned 50.

What did I do wrong?

What if I'm not good enough? Am I being punished?

What if I ate the wrong thing? What if I was exposed to something?

I eat right…well, pretty good most of the time.

Will the medicine make me sick?

Will I lose my hair?

I'm gonna die.

I don't have everything in order.

What's gonna happen to all of my *stuff*?

I need to get rid of *stuff*.

This isn't supposed to happen to me.

Did I catch something from all those people I've helped?

Glad we did that Canyon trip when we did.

Will I see my daughter graduate?

Will I get to help my son with his new house?

Marriages? Grandkids?

Will my family be okay?

Does God **really** love me?

Will He **really** heal me? Really?

I don't want to do this…

Heaven's a real place …

Just take me home!

AAAAAAAAAAAH! I cried out!

<Tears>

\<Tears\>

I cried some more.

This journey into uncharted territory was eerily familiar. Mom battled this same *dis-ease* for nearly 10 years. I had watched from the outside looking in. It wasn't a fun journey. Oh yes, she made the best of it, but it was agonizing. Especially when I scanned her 10-year battle for what I might be facing. Fatigue, pin pricks in her legs, burning sensations in her throat, *heat waves*, weakness, metallic tasting food, hair loss, shaky and numbness in her hands and that was just the first month of treatment. Medicine pumps, sleeplessness, restless legs, muscle soreness, indigestion, nausea, incontinence, ankles swelling, bone pain, hospitalizations, blood transfusions, stem cell transplants, energy loss, full time job going to the doc…and on it went and on and on. And then it was over. The memories were overwhelming.

I remembered the hard parts and it scared me.

I don't want to do this.

Just take me home!

Jesus help!

A friend sent a note, which included this…

> **I waited patiently for the Lord; He turned to me and heard my cry. He lifted me *up* out of the slimy pit of destruction, out of the mud and miry clay *of despair* and He set my feet upon a rock and gave me a firm place to stand** (Psalms 40:1-2 NIV/NASB – emphasis mine).

I haven't been patiently waiting for You, Lord.

I've been whining, complaining, stewing and fretting.

Did You really hear my cry?

Yes. I have heard you.

Will You really lift me up out of this slimy dark pit?

Please lift me up.

I need help!

I can't do this on my own.

I'm here with you.

Will I really be able to stand in the midst of all of this?

I'm a mess.

As I stood on this mental rock, I imagined all this mud oozing off of me.

I'm really a mess!

What if I can't handle this battle?

What's this all about?

It's not all about you.

I can use this...

Will you trust Me?

Yes! I think I will.

I love you!

I am with you...always!

Help me know...

Help me trust You.

God, I'll go through this if You go with me.

I'll go down this cancer road if You say so. I will fight to live and not give up. But only if **You get glory**! If not, cancel the plans of the enemy and take me home. God, I'll go through this if You go with me.

I'll get glory – if you share the story!

This IS a story, *His-story* that I get to share.

As I flipped through my Bible some more, it said:

> ...He (will) put a new song in my mouth, a song of praise to my God; many will see and fear and put their trust in the Lord (Psalms 40:3 NASB).

With the mud still dripping, things started turning around.

\<Deep breath\>

So, now on my mental Rock, my hands and face began to rise toward the skies and where I perceive my Lord to be.

We have a long journey ahead.

I will walk with you.

You are not alone.

I may not know what is next in this uncharted territory, but I know **Who** I am following and He has the map!

I'm in Your Good Hands.

I will go with You.

Please lead the way.

Help Along The Way

Yes, the cancer diagnosis was devastating, and yes, I descended into a dark, mucky place. Eventually, I did reach out to God. Funny thing, He had been there all the time. Things really were starting to turn around. Yes, I was still muddy, but my mental Rock brought confidence that I really wasn't alone, and God had given me help along the way. As I stood on my Rock, open to more insights and a better vantage point, some word pictures came into my mind and heart. Describing them, they become part of *His-Story*.

Fiery Furnace

The first one was of the fiery furnace mentioned in the Bible, where the three guys were thrown into that hot, fiery furnace, yet didn't get burned. They actually came out of the furnace with not even a *hint of smoke* on them. (See...No Smoke On Me)

Chemotherapy seemed like a type of fiery furnace so I adopted their phrase, "No smoke on me."

The Dolls

As I thought about other things that go into hot, fiery places, the second picture came to mind. It was of coal being formed into diamonds from the heat deep in the earth. The fire of chemotherapy may burn out the MM (Multiple Myeloma blood cancer) and anything else that shouldn't be there, but it can't touch the Diamond, the Diamond Girl.

The *Diamond Girl* is that part of me that is hidden deep inside. She is protected and saved because of what Jesus did on the cross. His death gave me His eternal life. The *Diamond Girl* will live forever, and death will not touch her no matter how sick my body becomes or how fearful my emotions get. Extreme heat and intense pressure makes for a beautiful gem. The *Diamond Girl* is strong. Chemotherapy can't touch the diamond! She is forever very much alive.

I am a very visual thinker. I love object lessons and word pictures. I needed to find a symbolic mascot. A hero for the battle! It needed to be something tangible that would remind me of how God would protect me in the fiery furnace of chemotherapy. Glass...crystal...Christmas ornament...I was looking everywhere and found nothing that worked.

Then I had an idea. I would make one. I bought a set of three nesting dolls. You know the ones made in Russia that fit inside of each other. I also bought a package of rhinestones and started gluing the little pieces all over the smallest, innermost doll. The *Diamond Girl* sparkled!

What about the other two?

The largest, outermost doll, I called the *Outside Girl.* She represented our physical body. During this time of discovery and waiting for decisions to be made about my health, we needed a distraction. My son, who had his own set of major health challenges, was visiting. So together, we decorated the *Outside Girl* with various things to represent the scars and bandages that each one of the "Cool Houles" had dealt with, including a couple of kidney beans and a stomach Band-Aid to represent my current challenge.

The *Middle Girl* was tricky. She sat for a long time, untouched. The solution came unexpectedly. I heard a young lady share a story about how God can take all the broken pieces of our life and put them together like a beautiful stained glass window. Okay, another train of thought. Why can't those broken pieces of glass be glued onto the *Middle Girl*? And so they were, with a little help from my sister-in-law, her glasscutter and fragments of glass. The *Glass Girl* was finished. My emotions did feel shattered. But there was hope. Hope that things could be put back together IF I would give God all the broken pieces.

I discovered that when you put additional pieces onto these little dolls, they no longer fit inside one another...bummer! After a quick dremmel-tool lesson, my brother- in-law handed me the solution to my dilemma. So with a bit of grinding of the inside surfaces, the *girls* were nesting back together.

This was quite a creative process and it was NOT done alone. There were others along the way that helped out, another picture for this season.

Looking back, I am thankful that I am not alone on this medical journey of uncharted territory. There are others along the way who helped out physically, mentally, emotionally, and spiritually. And I am grateful.

However, I am most grateful to Jesus for His death and resurrected life. He brings healing to the *Diamond Girl* from the *dis-ease* of sin and gives me the *ease* and hope of eternal life. **"By His stripes I am healed."** By the stripes and death of Jesus, my life, my eternal-everlasting life, has been healed from the unending death of Hell. And knowing that my *Diamond Girl,* my spirit, is safe and nothing can touch it, I can go through the tough times. I can stand on my Rock, even if my Outside Girl is falling apart.

There is a *Diamond Girl* or *Diamond Guy* in each of us...and nothing can touch the diamond!

Stomping

Some days I was fine walking along the path, in the uncharted territory. I actually skipped along at some points. Other days it felt like I was barely crawling. With all the uncertainties puzzling the doctors and occupying my focus, I found myself frozen and unable to function in my day-to-day life. It was like someone was waving their hands in my face and blocking every step I tried to take. My thoughts were interrupted and conversations often went back to medical questions and concerns. The situation seemed to bury me. I was *under the circumstances* and it was getting heavy. I REALLY DON'T LIKE being confined.

Then something started to rise up in me.

I was given *Strength*. The emotional turmoil and scary circumstances miraculously were put under foot. It didn't change the fact that the grim reality was still there, but the future was not my focus.

I may be in a battle, but I have places to go and things to do and people to love...life to live.

The mental discipline of "stomping" kept the situation under my feet, and stomping on it became a common phrase our family learned when Mom was in her battle with Multiple Myeloma.

We stomp on, keep under our feet, stomp out, destroy, and crush those things that don't belong. I guess you could call it a violent prayer.

Stomping: *The act of putting something under your feet in the authority of Jesus Christ and smashing it. Also, discovering that you are standing ON "it" and not under "it." This can include writing on the bottom of your shoe and dancing while singing praises to our King. In my case, Multiple Myeloma is written on the bottom of my shoes!!! Stomp ON! (A word from the virtual Cool Houle Family Dictionary)*

Feathered Hideout

As I went stomping along in this uncharted territory, I rediscovered something.

I call it my feathered hideout. It's a place where I can go to be alone.

A secret place.

A safe place.

 A shelter.

A fort.

Like a bird in its nest.

Only better. It's not an actual physical place but a mental, emotional place, a heart place. God meets me there. There isn't a secret password but the Words spoken seem to come from a Secret Source. There is Comfort and Peace. The meeting doesn't have an agenda but we do business, heart business.

Just Jesus and me.

I pour out my heart.

He listens.

I cry.

He reassures.

I am quiet.

I listen.

He encourages.

Sometimes He corrects.

Tweaks.

Comforts.

Brings hope.

Peace.

I am held in Good Hands.

Rescued

After hearing that a friend was also in a battle with cancer, I summarized what I had learned so far. I sent him this condensed version, hoping to encourage him with what I had discovered:

As the TV, computer, and cellphone screens are shut off, the noises are stilled, everyone returns to another place and the lights go out. I'm alone with myself in the inky darkness. Thoughts begin to wander. Fear is knocking on the door, along with doubt, worry, and self-pity. They have all come in against me like a flood, dragging me into the deep, mucky, miry pit. I am being emotionally kidnapped.

However, just as I am sinking in over my head, I feel a strong Hand reach out and rescue me out of the dark sinking hole. To my surprise, I find myself standing on a Solid Rock, dripping with mud. Somehow all those dark thoughts have dripped away, too, and cover the Rock I am now standing on.

As I lift up my head, I start to notice little things I hadn't seen before. Thankfulness, praise, and hope start to replace the dark thoughts. *"Peace comes in like a flood."* There is a song in my heart. I see the sky and the patterns in the clouds. My heart longs for what and **Who** is on the other side of that blue and white. Then there is this sweet awareness that I am not alone standing on this Solid Rock.

The Spirit is there. I can't see Him – but OH! I can feel Him. I can sense Him, like sunshine warming my skin. Now there is warmth on the inside, too.

Peace

Deep sigh

Relief, like I'm being hugged from the inside out.

AAAAHHHH!

The Spirit is lifting off heaviness, befriending me, comforting me, inviting me...

Come, Come follow Me.

He knows the Way. He IS THE Way.

He has a secret path for me to take. There are places to stop and rest, hiding places, amazing things to see and know, hard places – yet good. I am being refined and polished. It is in an uncharted territory where I learned to trust my Companion. He holds the map. There are treasures on this path.

In the shadows along the way, like a baby bird covered with the feathers of the parent wings, I am safe and secure.

Take good care my friend.

I Serve A Mighty God!

The Pits... To The Rock!

Dark Times... Yet Not Alone!

So Many Promises...

SECTION 2: FALL 2012

Problem Revealed

Summer into Fall

The email conversations will soon uncover more facts that you, Reader, have already discovered. The MM diagnosis, which at this point is still a mystery.

As we moved from summer into fall, tests were still being run to find out why my kidneys weren't working normally. But after spending time in my "feathered hideout", my attitude was much more positive. Life had been reordered and I was much more pleasant to be around.

I sent out more emails to keep family and friends in the loop.

📧 Sent: Thursday, September 20, 2012
📧 Subject: The Book–A Plan...to Stomp!

Hello Again,

Hope you are doing well.

The long story/details:

Jesus gives me authority, in His Name, to command things that don't belong to get out!!! And as we used to say as Mom went through her battle with cancer, we get to STOMP on all this stuff! Put it all UNDER my feet. We actually wrote things on the bottom of our shoes so we could STOMP all day. We saw things change. (Doctor's told her she had three months. She lived ten years!)

I've been collecting information over the last couple of days. Here's what I know:

Web:

Doctors and health advice pages should be avoided. (My husband peeked and said in a word, "DON'T." Just thought I'd pass that along.)

> Look UP!!! (And I don't mean online.)

Kidney:

> Biopsy NORMAL!!! YAY!!!
>
> No cancer in my Kidney, but abnormal function.
>
> Blood levels still *off*.
>
> Thick dense protein attaching to and clogging up kidneys (light-chain kidney *dis-ease**)
>
> *Fast growing unwanted cells, by definition is a cancer, this is NOT CANCER!!! (We found out later this *disease* is actually referred to as a *blood-cancer.*)

Kidney Plan:

> Lab continues to study biopsy cells under time and microscope.
>
> Final word Friday - not expected to change prognosis.
>
> More blood tests - to determine the exact protein being produced
>
> Body- x-ray to see if the proteins are attaching anywhere else
>
> Referral to specialist*

(*Oncologists monitor the medications (pills - series) that destroy these proteins. They use the same medications in more aggressive ways for more extreme situations.)

I will continue to be thankful for all that has been given to me and STOMP on those things that are trespassing.

By the way, if there is anything I can STOMP on for you, please let me know. I might not have very big feet but I can write small.

Thanks for listening to all of this.
STOMPING along!!!

In Good Hands,
Jeri

✉ Sent: September 26, 2012 9:46 PM
✉ Subject: Next chapter 9-26 Ford Factory

Good Evening,

It's a good day for ice cream!!! I'm actually eating it between thoughts and writing to you...yum.

The oncology doc was very straightforward and very suspicious of all the "proteins" collecting on my kidneys. (And for those of you that peeked at the WebMD, this won't be a surprise to you.)

He gave us an example: If you have a Ford Truck on every corner, you most likely have a Ford Factory nearby. We've got to find the factory and destroy it.

The protein factory, most likely, is **myeloma.** (Technically, no cancer cells found, just lots and lots of proteins. Too many of a good thing is NOT a good thing.)

To confirm his suspicion, he has ordered a bone marrow biopsy.

He also has a chemotherapy plan that could be implemented, if needed, by the end of next week.

Plan:

>Biopsy tomorrow morning
>
>Results and chemo plan next week

Stomping on!!!

Jeri

✉ Sent: Friday, October 5, 2012

✉ Subject: Next Chapter 10-5 Roller Coaster

Good Early Morning,

What a roller coaster ride. Puddle jumping with Kleenex in hand and *stomping* through sunshine.

More tests, including a bone marrow biopsy; phone appointments and being held real close. I'm learning things on this path, incredibly special things, that I wouldn't have learned anywhere else. I've faced the fear of my own death and been reminded to put the shovel down. There is *life to live*!!! *

The report is finally in. Waiting is one of the hardest parts. Oh, another patience lesson. The bone marrow has very low numbers of Myeloma/protein cells. That's good news. ** However, that makes it even more puzzling. Doc thought he'd see way more. (That's what 'stomping' can do for you. Thank you for your help with that!)

Plan:

> Focus on the kidneys - (operating at 25%).
>
> Start Chemotherapy Tuesday, Oct 9-low doses to kill the proteins that are clogging the filtering system (2x/week for 2 weeks then one week off, continue treatment until function returns).
>
> Stay in contact with Kidney Specialist.
>
> Continue *stomping*.
>
> Trusting Jesus to continue to show the way.

**FYI - Dr. "Oncology" will be presenting my case to a Lymphoma/Myeloma Conference to get some more opinions. The way I look at it, God gets more *press time* and we get to celebrate.

*I'm on my way to see our daughter in Ohio for a few days!!!! *Livin' Life!*
Thanks for listening.

In Good, Good Hands,

Jeri

No Smoke On Me

No Smoke on Me is based on a Bible story. In the story, a powerful, intimidating king ordered everyone to bow down and worship a huge idol that he had created. Three, God-worshiping men would not bow down. Their punishment was to be thrown into a fiery furnace. God rescued them from the fire. They were not hurt. The King and all the officials examined the men and were amazed and worshiped God. (Based on Daniel 3:13-28 NIV – paraphrase mine.)

The King of *Dis-ease* claims...

"If you do not worship, respect, give honor/homage to this idol of Multiple Myeloma you will be immediately cast, thrown, pitched into the midst of roaring, blazing, fiery furnace of Chemotherapy. What god, doctor, or treatment is there that can rescue or deliver you out of the power of my hands?"

I declare, "Your threat means nothing to me!!! I don't even need to give you an answer concerning this matter. IF you throw me into the furnace blazing with the fire of Chemotherapy, the GOD I serve is able to rescue me out of that roaring furnace. My God will rescue me out of your power of Multiple Myeloma and anything else you cook up, oh King of *Dis-ease*."

"BUT, even if He does not rescue me, let it be known to you, King of *Dis-ease*, it wouldn't make a bit of difference. I still won't bow down, serve, or focus on your god, doctor, or treatment. I will not worship, respect, give special honor or homage to this golden idol of Multiple Myeloma that you have set up. My heart is upright. I serve a Mighty God! He loves me. He is pleased with me. He is with me. It is my God that will uphold me and deliver me!!!"

The fiery furnace of Chemotherapy was heated up and I was thrown in, bound hand and foot.

However, in the midst of the fire I could be seen loosed, unharmed, walking freely about with Someone real shiny.

The King of *Dis-ease* called out, "Come out here! Come out, servant of the Most High God!!!"

All the important people, officials, doctors, Lymphoma/Myeloma Conference members and counselors all gathered around. They examined my test results. They examined me and discovered that the fire of Chemotherapy had no ill effect on my body. My hair stayed in place, my skin and organs were not touched, **and there wasn't even the smell of smoke on me.** The fire of Chemotherapy burned the powerful binding ropes of Multiple Myeloma.

My God was blessed. He sent His angels to rescue me. I put my trust in Him. I laid my body on the line rather than worship Chemotherapy or Multiple Myeloma. My heart remained upright!

No smoke on me!

✉ Sent: Wednesday, October 10, 2012
✉ Subject: Next Chapter 10-10-12   Chemo Begins/Fiery Furnace

Good late morning,

Wow! Lots can happen in a week's time. Real highs, some lows, but leveling out nicely.

Had a wonderful trip to Ohio to see our daughter and her Ohio family (roommate and her family).

I'm discovering an amazing support system that is all around me; special hugs, sunshine walks, short messages, songs, root work, taxi services, flowers, tomatoes, emails, cards, prayers, stories, even the quiet -"*I'm not sure what to say, but I'm reading your story*" supporters. Thanks so much!!!

Medical Treatment begins: 10-9-12

I may be walking into the fiery furnace of chemotherapy but like Shadach, Meshach and Abednego, I won't be burned 'cause there is Someone REAL shiny with me. (Daniel 3)*

Believing for the Multiple Myeloma, extra proteins, to be burned.

Plan:

Injections at the doc's office: 21 day cycle (Tuesday/ Friday - 2 weeks on/1 week off)

Repeat until kidneys are functioning better.

Pills at home

Side effects: They have told me everything that might happen. Scary stuff. But, then said, "It should be minimal." I'm believing for no burning, not even the hint of smoke*. (See above reference to the story in Daniel)

Sleep is a good thing.

Naps are good, too. Eat well, exercise, laugh.

(I added that last one, it's good medicine.)

Bottom line: The next phase of this battle has begun. The good news, I win, regardless of the conditions!!!!

It's what I trust in, but don't see YET, that keeps me going.

Thanks for listening!

Stomping,

Jeri

📧 Sent: Saturday, October 20, 2012

📧 Subject: Next chapter 10-20-12 Numbers in Half/ Happy Dance

We're doin' the "Happy Dance" around here.

Last week's blood tests showed that the light chain protein levels, aka Multiple Myeloma, had been cut in half. Thank you Jesus.

Dr. Onc just happened to walk through the treatment room on Friday and spoke to us. He was pleased, too.

Doubts that God might not want to be helping *me*, wiped out.

Lies replaced by the truth; He loves me. He's got me in His Hands and is in control.

<Deep breath>

He gets the shine!

Fire all around, no smoke on me!

Round 1: Finished chemo treatment on Friday. This next week is considered my "off week." I was trying to be funny and said it was our "ketchup" week or maybe it's a mustard week or mayo week. My husband said, "I think it's our Miracle-Whip week."

We are definitely in the right atmosphere for miracles to be whipped up.

Thank you Jesus.

Stomping,

Jeri

✉ Sent: Monday, November 12, 2012

✉ Subject: next chapter 11-11-12 Stomped Defined/Quill Pen

Welcome to the continuing saga.

As a friend told me this weekend, "You are a *quill pen* God will use to write *His-story*." As long as Jesus gets the shine and glory, I will continue to share.

Round 2: Finished Chemotherapy on Friday and now another week off!!!

The numbers have not changed much in any direction. Steady as she goes and *stomping* along the way!

Round 3: Starts Monday, Nov. 19, appointment with Dr. Oncology

Next injection on Tuesday, Nov 20.What is changing is my inside perspective. I continue to face insecurities and fears, however, every time something threatens me, *reassurance* is right around the corner. Here's one example: I have been concerned with gaining weight with this medicine. I was gently reminded that my value and worth is NOT in my appearance. The doc has told me to keep my weight up. The nurse on Friday, who gave me my injection, said he was not used to working with *a lean machine model*. My husband and I chuckled at the timing of this "gentle-man's" words.

I am feelin' good. I have all my hair, stomach is settled, head is clear, and was told, "you don't look sick." I don't feel sick. I enjoy naps on some days, pace myself, and can keep up for the most part.

My husband and I participated in a Marriage Conference at the Coast this weekend. What an amazing *filling-up of my bucket* from many different sources. There was even a *sunshine* walk on the beach. Thank you, Jesus.

In the words of the Physician's Assistant I saw two weeks ago, I am doing "Phenomenal, Miraculous"!!! I am thankful.

Thanks for listening and stomping,

In Good Hands,

Jeri

✉ Sent: Wednesday, November 21, 2012
✉ Subject: Next Chapter 11-21-12   The Bells/Thanksgiving

So many things to be thankful for, and yes, I know it is the theme for the week, but I'm working on making it a habit.

Dr. Onc was very pleased Monday, with the way things are going.

"You are doing very well!"

He also said this is a marathon and not a sprint and gave me Friday off! (For the holiday.) Yeah!

Round 3: started Tuesday 11-20-12. "Goin' for the knock out punch!"...Of the *bad guys*, aka, the Multiple Myeloma (MM) cells that are doing the damage. And the *good guys* aka, healthy cells, kicked back on the blood tests. Everything is going in the right direction. Thank you, Jesus. And thanks to Mom and Pop for blazing a trail before me.

Thank you for all your support that comes in so many ways: stomping prayers, glove box cookies, cards, emails, songs, chats, rides, unspoken thoughts, your stories, hugs, "funnies", lunch, meals, treats, even "stomping grounds" coffee mugs, now with a whole new meaning. I am blessed.

Being thankful...Praising.

I read in the Bible that David, considered *a man after God's heart*, praised the Lord seven times a day. So, wanting to be a *woman after God's heart*, I figured out that if I set an alarm on my phone on the even hours between 8:00am to 10:00pm, that the bells would ring seven times and remind me to think thankfully. It also helps remind me that I am not alone and that He loves me. (Ps119: 164-165 NASB paraphrase mine.) One day at a time!

Hug your family a little tighter,

Full of THANKS!

Jeri

Sifted Like Wheat!

Facing The Challenge.
Oh It's Black!!!

Find The Treasures
In The Storm!

He Delivered Me
From My Fears!

There's
Always
Hope!

SECTION 3: WINTER 2012

Doubts

Storms

We weren't in the Grand Canyon during the stormy season, but were told that it can be treacherous. The rains cause the river to rise, sending mud into the water as it washes into the Canyon. The river becomes a mudflow. Storms can come up without notice, sending even the hardiest traveler scrambling for some type of shelter. The weather in this medical uncharted territory was also unpredictable. When this emotional storm of Multiple Myeloma started, I invited people to start praying for me. And, as I mentioned earlier, in our family praying had become synonymous with "stomping."

So we started stomping. And we found out that there were "Stomping Grounds" all over the country!

Yes, it was very reassuring to know I wasn't alone in this journey that had quickly become a raging storm. Many responded with amazing love and support, and I scrambled under their shelter:

We'll have faith, when yours is weak.

Stomping!

Keep us posted – we're stomping.

Praying with all my heart! I'm sending you lots of love your way. Take a deep breath and take in all this, one day at a time.

Keep me informed and know, my dear friend, I pray for you

EVERY day even if I don't write.

I love you, my friend! I'll keep praying!

We're praying! Much love and concern.

My thoughts and prayers are with you and your family as you get more information and a plan of care from your doctors.

I can't wait to see what He's going to do with this one.

Thanks for the update; we will be stomping with you.

I pray that through this section of your journey you will learn to trust Him more.

We do have a celebration ahead of us no matter the outcome of our battle on earth.

I have dug out my stomping shoes and will stomp and stomp and stomp!

And that's just a few of the comments!

The encouragement poured in!

Yet the storms came anyway. I questioned. I wondered. I cried. I tried to stay busy. I tried to *run away and hide* from those big black clouds that were heading my direction. On one of those days I actually stepped off the *uncharted path*, climbed into the *feathered hideout* all by myself and got settled. Then, I had a heart-to-heart chat with God.

God, what's going on?

Why are we in this place?

Are you really there?

What are you doing?

I'm feeling attacked.

Help!!!

I opened up my Bible to a verse that I had read before:

> "Simon, Simon, behold, Satan has demanded
> permission to sift you like wheat; but I have
> prayed for you, that your faith may not fail;
> and you, when once you have turned again,
> strengthen your brothers" (Luke 22:31-32
> NASB).

This time five words popped out at me…

<Deep breath>

> "I have prayed for you."

I read it from different versions.

> Did I read that right?
>
> If He would pray for Simon in the Bible story, does that
> mean He has also prayed for me in my story?
>
> Hmmm?

I figured this Multiple Myeloma journey-storm was a sifting of wheat, a sifting of me.

So I inserted my name into the story…and smiled.

> "(Jeri), (Jeri), behold, Satan has demanded
> permission to sift you like wheat; but I have
> prayed for you, that your faith may not fail;
> and you, when once you have turned again,
> strengthen your brothers" (Luke 22:31-32
> NASB- emphasis mine).

Marching orders:

> "Jeri, Satan has demanded permission and
> tried his best to sift and separate you from me,
> like chaff from wheat. But…

> I have prayed for you...
> that you would not give in or give out, that
> your faith would not fail. And once you have
> come through this time of testing and turned
> back to health, you would strengthen your
> companions, friends, family, brothers and
> sisters and give them encouragement and a
> fresh start (Luke 22:31-32 NASB, MSG, NIV -
> my paraphrase).

Jesus has prayed for me!!! He prayed that my faith would not fail. He did not pray I would not go through some tough times, but that my faith would not fail IN the tough times.

I would like to say that this is where the emotional storm ended and that I found the silver lining. But I cannot. The dark clouds continued to surround me. I snuggled down even further into the *feathered hideout* and cried out...

Somehow I knew it would get worse before it would get better.

My faith would not fail...? Really?

It feels pretty shaky.

Do you really love me?

Are you really there?

One minute I felt confident I'm not alone and then the next question if it's really true.

I'm not good enough.

I can help others, but ...can I?

I'm finished.

I'm so tired.

Tough times, I've seen them. I've watched others go through them. I've gone through my share…haven't I?

Father, if You are willing, remove this from me. I don't want to go through this.

Sigh

Tears

I'll just go *home* now. Just take me.
Can't this be over now?

Oh it's black!!!

Make another choice. Put on a happy face.

This storm will pass.

Keep watching for the treasures.

Maybe even a rainbow.

The *bells* are ringing.

What am I thankful for?

Even wheat is NOT thrashed forever…

Sent: Saturday, December 15, 2012
Subject: Next Chapter 12-15-12 Storm Clouds/Plateau

Hi There,
Hope you are well, anticipating…it's Christmas!
Christmas changes everything!!!

Round 4: Started Tuesday 12-11-12.

Blood work is holding steady. Dr. Onc said, "Plateaued."

That's not what I wanted to hear! However, as a friend pointed out, "It may not be any better, but it's NOT any worse!!!"

The nurses in the treatment room handed me the lab results and commented on the Kappa light chain numbers along with corresponding Lambda numbers saying, we're waiting for a Delta. (Delta is a scientific phrase for change.) "Delta of the Kappa and Lambda, it's beginning to sound like a college sorority."

We laughed!

Ready for Delta!!!

Dr. Kidney checked in this week, too. She was very reassuring, saying we should see changes with this Round 4 or Round 5. The kidney function and the MM will mirror each other. Meaning that as the MM counts improved we would see the kidney function also improve.

We will see Delta.

I have discovered that whatever treatment lies ahead, and whenever "remission" arrives, I can keep the April/May dates on the calendar that will celebrate college graduation for our daughter in Ohio. Yay!!!!

In the mean time, I'm living life, one day at a time, with: sweet ballets, gingerbread houses in glass buildings, Yahtzee, Christmas gatherings and decorations, surprises, refrigerator magnets, quiet thoughts from afar, car trips, shared hobbies, castle tours, ice cream, frozen cake, chats, meals, hugs, baby elephants, music, notes, pictures, cards, shopping, canned foods en masse...stomping team! Oh yes, Kleenex too, cause I never know when even the happy tears will come leaking out!

Thanks for the part that you play!

In really Good Hands,

Jeri

Stomping/prayer in a nutshell....

*DELTA!

*He continues to get the glory.

*Blood counts -change/improve.

*Kidney function - improve.

*Multiple Myeloma counts - go down.

*Continue to live in The PEACE He gives for today.

*Use energy wisely.

Storm Delta

I went through a storm that brought lots of *wind and rain* after a Multiple Myeloma Educational/Informational Seminar. The presenter did a one-hour fly-by over the big picture of this liquid cancer *dis-ease*. It was way more information than I had really allowed myself to process. She called it **cancer**. She was talking about the long term progression of the *dis-ease* and used words and definitions that felt like a punch in the gut. I'm sure it's good information to have. I am informed, even more now. However, we're not even sure what my individual case will look like down the road. So, I choose not to live fearing what might be ahead.

That choice, to not get too far ahead of things, came a few days after this seminar. It was during my *rest week*, as I walked down a quiet country road in Eastern Oregon. I had to face a big black cloud of possible future outcomes.

I came to a stop sign and literally and emotionally turned around.

The sky was changed.

My attitude was changing!

These clouds, that I now faced, were wispy in the morning light and the pinkish, orange colors were very encouraging.

"Refocus!!!"

I *stomped* my way back to the house through the puddles left from the storm, dried my eyes, and decided to live each day I have in front of me, one at a time. Even the horses that were frolicking in the fields earlier were waiting for me at the fence line, seeming to say,

"Did you hear Him? Refocus, play, live your life!"

Darkest just before the Delta.

Ohhhh! The double rainbows were amazing on the way back home!

There really are treasures in the storm!

Bridges

Storms bring black clouds.

Black clouds bring rain.

Rain brings rising water.

Rising waters bring floods.

Floods need bridges.

Those bridges allow me to cross the emotional murky waters. But they also allow others to cross over, bringing courage and comfort to rescue me.

It's going to be okay.

We're still praying and stomping for you and your family.

It might be different but we'll start new traditions.

You're not alone.

I'll be there.

It's going to be okay. (I must have really needed to hear this one!)

You have the authority of Christ living in you. Use it!!!

You look beautiful.

Let's live life...take a nap if you need to.

I sought the Lord and He answered me, and delivered me from all my fears (Psalms 34:4 NASB).

Held...

Tears...

Tissues

Comfort

Can I bring you dinner?
Wanna go for a ride?
It's going to be okay.

On a journey like this, it would be easy to stay focused on the storm, black clouds, rising water, and hold on to your hat for what comes next. I have to be honest. I have my moments: tests, waiting for results, strange medicines, deepening fatigue, scattered thoughts, sensations causing alarm, learning a new normal, even conversations that bring worry and fear, tears. However, knowing there is a bridge of hope crossing to higher ground is a good thing. I know the storm won't last and the flood will subside. Promises from my Lord that I am not alone help too; He is with me and He loves me. Even if the rainbow is hiding.

In the Grand Canyon, there is a suspension bridge over the Colorado River that allows hikers and mule riders into the deepest part of the canyon. The ranch at the very bottom is like an oasis for the weary, hot, parched travelers. The hope of shade and a cool drink at the ranch brings relief, even to the river floaters. The bridge brings in needed supplies for those who remain at the remote ranch and for those on foot, gives access back up to higher ground.

Bells

You, the reader, may have *heard the bells* in an earlier email. Here is the rest of that story. One of the biggest *attitude adjustments* came from setting an alarm on my phone. The alarm sounded like church bells. I don't think the sound of the alarm was significant at the time, but the consistency of it changed me. It reminded me to cross the bridge from the negative dark thoughts to the positive higher thoughts. The alarm helped turn things around, get me out of the emotional pits, refocus, think about something else, stomp, and keep all this medical stuff under my feet. It was a good reminder. When the bells rang, I chose to be thankful and re-secured my Lifejacket.

It all started as I remembered a story I'd heard about a man in the Bible. I looked it up. The Bible says,

> **"...I have found David...a man after My**
> **(God's) own heart, who will do all My will"**
> (Acts 13:22 NASB).

He wanted to know God. He loved God and even though he made mistakes in his life, God loved him. God crossed a bridge reaching out to David. David reached back.

I want a relationship like that with God. I wondered, "What did David do that turned his heart towards God?" One thing that stands out to me is that he praised God. He was thankful.

> **"Seven times a day I *(David)* praise you..."**
> (Psalms 119:164 NIV).

David praised The Lord seven times a day. So, wanting to be a *woman after God's own heart*, I did the math. I figured out that if I set an alarm on my phone every two hours between 8:00am to 10:00pm, the *bells* would ring seven times and remind me to think thankfully. It also reminds me that I am not alone and that He loves me.

I choose to be thankful even if the healing is delayed.

I choose to stay positive and thankful. It seemed to help.

I believe that God has a plan beyond what I can see. I will trust Him.

This alarm system worked out really well, especially since it was in November (2012) when I started it. The bells rang, others heard it and wondered what was going on. It was easy to explain. There were lots of *thankfuls*. It was contagious!!!

Happy Thanksgiving; happy giving of thanks!!! Everyday! All the time!

I must say, however, on a stormy day when those bells rang, it was a challenge to praise. Sometimes I just didn't feel like it, but it was a choice. And yes, sometimes I just turned it off, but most of the time I could find something to be thankful for and the day went a little better. And as the journey continued, the bells were also a reminder the doctor wanted me to drink lots of water for my kidneys and use the restroom frequently. With all that water, I really didn't need to be reminded of the latter.

✉ Sent: Monday, December 31, 2012 - New Years Eve

✉ Subject: Next Chapter 12-31-12 New Meds/Roller Coaster

Happy New Years Eve....

What a roller coaster ride. I usually close my eyes and hang on tight as the *emotional car* zooms down the track waiting for it to level out. It's in this leveling out phase that you usually hear from me. However, I am realizing that this *story writing business* is also part of my treatment/processing. So thanks again for coming along for the ride. So, now, as the story continues, my stomach is in my throat....

I heard from Dr. Onc the week of Christmas and saw one of

the *team doctors* today. Nobody likes the resistant plateau where the numbers of my blood tests seem to be hovering.

With that being the case, there are other options. So, beginning tonight, I will start another drug* in addition to the injections/pills.

They had to talk me through all the side effects and possibilities. Not fun, not fun to think about. But as the doc said, "All small potatoes compared to MM."

Good perspective.

And the good news: I have my hair, a new pair of glasses for my tired eyes, and I'm not pregnant! (Seriously, I must take frequent pregnancy tests, by law, in order to take this new medicine.)

We should start to see results, **Delta**, within the month. What will this new combination of medicine do? Hopefully **punch the "lights" out of the chain!!!**

One of the tests/numbers is called "the free light-chain protein" aka: Multiple Myeloma, liquid cancer, cancer of the plasma. The free light-chain is divided into two parts, Kappa and Lambda. The **Delta** change, is what we are waiting to see.

My case is unusual and is not following *Standard Operating Procedures*. I am unique, one of a kind, on lots of levels!!!

Dr. Onc reminds me that he's very good at what he does, and he has people to help him. So, as my questions come up, he reassures me that I can ask. **My** list of questions is **his** list. He wants me to know and understand what's going on. So I ask!

The ride's not over, but my seat belt and helmet are back in place. I've had lots of hugs, replacement Kleenex in the car, stomping on a treadmill in the corner that replaced the wilting Christmas tree, warm bed, toasty fire, messages, hand sanitizer/soap-water, Christmas reminders, road trip, sappy movies, games, family time....

I think I need to find a real live roller coaster and have fun with it! It's on my list. And when I finish that, I'll add something else, a never-ending, never-finished *life list*.

As much as I appreciate the doctors, all their reassurance and advancements in medicine, I continue to put my trust in Jesus and all He can do!!!

Keep your sunny-side up!

In Good Hands,

Jeri

*Revlimid; a derivative of Thalidomide. A sleeping pill used in Germany a long time ago that caused horrible birth defects. They aren't taking any chances of pregnancy. I should sleep great!!!!

Jesus said...

"But the Counselor, the Holy Spirit, whom the Father will send in My name, will teach you all things and will remind you of everything I have said to you. Peace I leave with you; my peace I give you. I do not give to you as the

**world gives. Do not let your hearts be troubled
and do not be afraid,**" (JOHN 14:26–27 NIV).

Thanks for listening!

✉ Sent: Thursday, January 03, 2013
✉ Subject: Next "mini" Chapter 1-3-13 Happy Dance #2

Hi there,

Time for another "Happy Dance"!!!!

We got some test results at treatment today:

The Free-Light-Chain Protein (Multiple Myeloma) is down from 253.3 to 161.3!!!!!

Delta has happened. The goal is 15. We are moving in the right direction. And this test was done **before** the new med was started. It should really drop now.

BTW, the new med routine is going well, too.

Thanks for your stomping!

In Good Hands,

Jeri

✉ Sent: Wednesday, January 9, 2013
✉ Subject: Next Chapter 1-9-13 Storm Drain/Clogged Kidneys

It's me again....

Thank you for allowing me to interrupt your day. This is a good outlet.

Monday at treatment the nurse handed us the report card, aka: blood test results. The kidney function numbers* were climbing the wrong direction.

WHAT?

What does that mean?

What did I do wrong?

What can I change to make it go the right way?

Is this new medicine the right decision?

The MM count improved so much. I thought the kidney function would follow. What's going on?

So many questions, fear and worry creeping in.

HOLD ON! WHO is in control here?

Obviously not me, but it took me a few days to get back on track.

My Jesus is still in control.

In my weakness, He is strong.

However, my stomping looked more like hobbling, at best; more like a limp.

You did NOTHING wrong!!!

Celebrate the good news and don't overreact to the other.

Keep drinking lots of water.

Stay positive.

The enemy has been defeated.

Claim your victory.

Great words of encouragement came from all around me.

Both Dr. Onc and Dr. Kidney added their reassurance....

"The new combination of medicine should be more

effective to get you all the way into remission."

"The kidneys are often slackers and the myeloma protein falls before the kidneys start to improve"...

Whew!!!!! Okay...that feels better.

The kidney-Myeloma combination is much like the storm drain after a big wind/rain storm. The gutters are full of water, but the drain is clogged with all the leaves and rubble that have blown into the street. It takes a big stick, heavy-duty medicine to move the debris, Myeloma, out of the way. It takes a while, but eventually the water, the kidney function starts working again. With remission of the Myeloma, the kidneys should repair themselves.

Patience!!! Endurance!!! Trust!!!

What do you do on the roller coaster ride, as a sudden twist occurs? When the car comes to the top of the ramp, just on the brink of going over the edge...Hold on tight OR let go and lift your hands? I am choosing to let go, lift my hands and shout!!! "THANK YOU, JESUS!!!"

I'm still looking for a real live roller coaster!!!

Peace!!!!

With a bit of reminding, I am learning to

> Sit - with The Lord and BE - before I try to do.
>
> Walk - with the grace He gives - then I can
>
> Stand - against the enemy and all that he tries to throw my way. [8]

Thanks for listening,

In Good Hands,

Jeri

Life with Jesus is not immunity from difficulties,
but PEACE in difficulties. (Russell)

✉ Sent: Monday, January 28, 2013
✉ Subject: Next Chapter 1-28-13 Quick update/Watch the Trend

Two steps forward, one step back...is still one step forward. Delta - change.

Light Chain count up from 161 to 178...

Dr. Onc says, "Watch the overall trend more than each individual test." (Good idea) "The treatment you're on now is much more likely to drive the Light Chains to normal and give your kidneys a chance to repair themselves." (I like that!)

"We'll wait it out. Give this new medicine three rounds before making any judgments." (In the middle of second round of the new combo)

Light Chain up from 161 to 178...but down from 558. (Nice trend)

Recovering from a staff infection in my right nostril. ????? What? Crazy stuff!!!

Enjoying dinners with/from friends, new recipes to try, walks, skies filled with thousands of geese, squirrels, birds, country drives, amazing pictures, creative projects, future plans, emails, cards, calls, team shopping, unspoken thoughts and prayer/stomping...thanks for all the support!

In Good Hands,
Jeri

✉ Sent: Thursday, January 31, 2013
✉ Subject: Next Chapter 2-1-13 More Tests...Drink More Water, too!

Hello Again,

The report card: blood test results, received on Tuesday showed the kidney function, aka Creatinine number, is up again...now at 2.88. The nurse who gives my treatment prints the results off but doesn't really say anything about it.

Questions mounting; doctor questions. I've been told if I have questions, to ask. So I did...

"Dr. Onc, are you concerned about the 2.88 Creatinine number, up again, from 2.52?" Seems he was, and so was Dr. Kidney. They had been talking amongst themselves. More tests and blood work have been ordered to determine if there is something else going on with the kidneys. They both said, "Drink more water!" So as I go floating along, we shall see.

Kidney ultra sound on Friday 2-2-13

Blood/Urine test on Tuesday 2-5-13

Double Doc Appointment Monday 2-11-13 (Dr. Onc/Dr. Kidney)

I feel good. Conserve energy, take naps, eat well, bake cookies, drink lots of water, and walk. I may be in the fiery furnace, but there's no smoke on me!

We're stomping!!! Thanks for stomping along!

In Good Hands,

Jeri

Sent: Wednesday, February 06, 2013

Subject: Next Chapter 2-6-13 Preliminary Report/Good News

Hello Again,

I was relieved when I heard this, so I'd like to pass the news along to you.

While I did get all the tests and ultra sounds completed as asked, I also went in to see a Physicians Assistant for a swollen, painful finger. I probably just bumped it on something, but with Chemo you have to be so careful with everything. Crazy, weird things can quickly become a concern. She put me on antibiotics and has me soaking it in Epson Salts. It's better today!

Also, while I was with Doc PA, who was very positive and reassuring, she opened up the clinician's notes about my Ultra Sound and let me peek!

Bottom Line: Ultra Sound - no change. That's good news!!!

Creatinine Levels – DOWN to 2.57 from 2.88!!! I guess all that water really does make a difference. That's good news too.

Kappa Light Chains results aren't in, yet.

Next:

Monday 2-11-13: Double Appointments with Dr. Onc and Dr. Kidney. They will both have additional comments about all the test and scans.

Tuesday 2-12-13: Start Round 7 Velcade/Round 3 Revlimid

Enjoying a *rest week*. I even went to my first Opera this

weekend. There were subtitles above the stage on a reader board. Fun times! Major points for my husband who, unknowingly bought tickets in November on the same day as the Super Bowl. The timing for the day was pretty good though. We got home in time to see the blackout, which occurred at the stadium, and the second half of the game. The best of both!!!

Thanks for Stomping!

Keep finding the treasures...they are there!

In Good Hands,

Jeri

Clearing Skies

Life really is unpredictable like the weather. There comes a time in the storms where the sky begins to clear. Black clouds, wind and rain give way to sun breaks, puddles drying and occasionally even rainbows. There are seasons where multiple storms race through the sky on a daily basis.

When the *numbers* being watched head in the wrong direction, more unanswered questions arise and more tests are ordered. I wonder if I did something that caused the change.

Dark clouds.

What are they going to find this time?

Doubts.

Will I be able to survive all these tests and treatments?

Am I going to get sick?

Is this the right treatment?

Maybe I shouldn't take the chemo at all.

Is my hair going to fall out?

Did I drink enough water?

Worry.

Is it getting worse?

What are they going to tell me?

Am I gonna be sick like Mom?

I don't want my family to go through this.

Is it gonna hurt?

Will this be the end?

Did I pray enough?

Did I pray the right prayers?

Did Jesus change His mind?

Waiting.

Waiting...

for results.

But oh, the deep relief when things turn around.

The skies begin to clear.

The sun streams through the remaining clouds, shining a ray of hope into my day.

My attitude gets adjusted.

Thanks for *what is*, replaces fears of the *what ifs*.

Thank You for my kidneys working at 20% without dialysis.

Thank You for my doctors being on top of things.

Thank You for my hair and eye lashes and eye brows.

Thank You that I don't look sick.

Thank You for a warm house and a warm bed for naps.

Thank You for a treatment plan and insurance to cover

the costs.

Thank You for allowing me to be at home.

Thank You for my husband and his support and encouragement.

Thank You for my loving kids.

Thank You for my friends and family and the outpouring of support.

Jesus, thank You for holding on to me.

No matter what the storm clouds bring, I can cry out. He (God) can handle it. And He knows where I walk in this uncharted territory! He knows my every thought. He clears the skies. I am in Good Hands.

Sent: Tuesday, February 12, 2013

Subject: Next Chapter 2-12-13 Doctors Chime In/Confirmed Improvement

Good Afternoon,

I think it is important to celebrate the little victories along the way, so it's time to get the "happy dancin" shoes on!!!

Bottom line: The numbers are all going in the right direction this week!!! Thank You, Jesus! Thank you for stomping!!!

I saw both Dr. Onc and Dr. Kidney yesterday....

Dr. Onc said that one line of thinking in the oncology world is that when a patient is slow to improve that is takes a longer time to get worse again. * We keep making progress on the slow side, which isn't a bad thing. The overall trend is good. And he wants to get the lowest numbers possible.

His parting words to me were, "Keep your alert on high and check with us on the little things, they can get out of hand. People won't know you are sick. You look healthy and your hair is full. You are a star patient. Keep up the good work." (My swollen finger is back to normal! A little strange thing.)

*Multiple Myeloma is the kind of dis-ease that you punch down into remission and hope that it stays there for a long time before it rears its ugly head again. They don't have a cure at this point, but a maintenance plan. And we have Jesus and ultimately He gets to decide.

Dr. Kidney reviewed the ultra sound and said that things did look good:

> no blockage
>
> no stones
>
> no mass
>
> no infection
>
> no reaction

However, they noticed that the kidneys get swollen as the bladder fills and then shrink again when the bladder is empty...puzzling. So, the doctor would like to do another test to make sure there is no blockage between the two organs. It is possible that the fibroids that I have in the uterus could be causing the blockage. We'll find out.

Test: This Friday - 90 minutes.

She also said if there is no blockage, she is content to wait. (Time and patience) "The kidneys are probably waiting for the burden of the light chains (MM) to clear out."

Here's another place to celebrate. Even though my kidneys are operating at about 20%, my body is functioning well. Let's just say I am comfortable and flowing fine!!! Our bodies are amazing creation machines!

The *bell alarms* that I started in November to be thankful are now also a reminder to drink water and clear my bladder. And if I wait too long, I'll be doin' a little dance for another reason...!

Thanks for listening.

In Good Hands

Jeri

📧 Sent: Tuesday, February 19, 2013

📧 Subject: Next Chapter 2-19-13 Stars On The Screen/No Blockage

Hello there,

Dr. Kidney and I connected today.

Bottom line: The Mag3 Radioactive Test* that they ran on my kidneys Friday showed NO BLOCKAGE! Yeah!!!

"Perfect flow" was the Doc's comment.

Thank You, Jesus! Thank YOU for stomping!!!

The Free Light Chains (MM) are checked every three weeks. No news on that one. Good trend continues.

The Creatinine levels are doing their yo-yo tricks, back up from 2.50 to now 2.57. Dr. Kidney's comment was from the beginning, "We will probably see the Creatinine numbers drop when the (MM) Free Light Chains are cleared out. Patience!!! And even if your normal is in the 2.5-ish range, you could live your life without having to be on dialysis." However she would like to see the numbers lower! Me, too!!! "We will keep watching the labs."

So in the meantime, I have enjoyed 50 red roses. This is my 50th year, Jubilee!!! Also: walks in the pre-popping spring, visit to the Japanese Garden, *playing* in my yard and flowerbeds, yes, there is a bit of color showing under all those newly raked up leaves, celebrating with our son, his future house closing in a few days, preparing for a trip to Ohio for our daughter's senior project and graduation, and of course drinking LOTS of water!!! Rides to and from places, special meals, cards, emails, thoughts, and prayers. The support all seems to come at just the right time, too. I'm so thankful.

*Mag3 - Radioactive Medicine Test. After injecting the material into my vein through an IV, I lay on a camera-table. There was a screen that I could see from this prone position that showed my mid-section. At first it looked like a dark *sky, filled* with tiny little *stars*. The technician told me it was the radioactive dye in my blood stream. As I continued to watch, those *stars* began to concentrate in my kidneys. All of a sudden I could see the outline of my left and right kidney, and the *sky* became less *star struck*. As the 45 minutes wore on, the bright, *star-filled* kidneys started to spill a stream of *stars* towards the bottom of the screen. I then realized, that my bladder was now filling up with *stars* and the bladder outline was now clear. At the buzzer of this test and a trip to the restroom, all that water I'd been drinking helped move the *stars* right out of my system.

In my untrained, unofficial opinion, there was NO blockage!!! And that was confirmed today!!!

Enjoy the little things.

In Good Hands,

Jeri

📧 Sent: Thursday, March 07, 2013

📧 Subject: Next Chapter 3-7-13 Steady Trend/Downward!

Just a quick note....

Bottom line: MM - Light Chain counts continue the downward trend...yeah! Down to 95.7 from 102.9 at the last check.

Creatinine is still wiggling back and forth, patience.

I was reminded this week that Multiple Myeloma has multiple ways that it presents itself. And depending on how it is presenting, different blood tests are used to track the proteins. It can all be confusing, especially if you know someone else that has MM and the things they are following don't match with what I've been talking about.

In my case we are following the Light Chain protein levels.

Lovin' the sunshine

In Good Hands,

Jeri

Can Anything
Good Come
Of This?

HOPE!

PEACE!

Feathered Hideout...
Look Close!

Arise...
Let's Go On
From Here...

Prep for...False Alarm

Rainbows

Oh yes, it's been black. Yes, there have been clearing skies. And yes, there are *rainbows of hope* peeking through...
From my feathered hideout I hear...

> *Jeri – I love you.*
>
> *I'm here for you.*
>
> *Keep trusting Me.*
>
> *I will comfort you.*
>
> *I do have your days numbered, but I have plans for you, here.*

You do not realize now what I am doing, but later you will (JOHN 13:7 NIV).

> *I have more to teach you.*
>
> *I have more to show you.*
>
> *I have things I need you to do.*

I will instruct you and teach you in the way which you should go;

I will counsel you with My eye upon you.
(PSALMS 32:8 NASB).

(I will) preserve you from trouble and...

surround you with songs of deliverance (PSALMS 32:7 NASB).

Keep walking with Me on this secret path.

I have treasures to show you.

<Deep breath...>

Double rainbows.

Can anything good come out of this?

God, can You get glory out of this?

I'll go down this road if You say so. I will fight to live and not give up. But only if You get glory! If not, cancel the plans of the enemy and take me home. God, I'll go through this if You go with me.

I will get the glory if you keep telling the story.

I know you can heal me. Help me with my unbelief.

I am here with you.

Not my ways, but Yours!!!

(I would repeat these last few phrases many times on this journey as I wavered back and forth.)

And WHEN I have gone through it, I WILL turn back to help and encourage others if You show me how.

We'll get to that later.

At the moment, I was beginning to feel at rest and at peace like my feathered friends must feel when they sit warm and comfortable, high above the roar, in the security of their nest. With the chaos all around, they hunker down and trust that they are in Good Hands.

These word pictures became another way for me to stay focused on God's peace. Keeping my hands busy with getting it down on paper also helped. So many doodles, so many stories to share.

"Arise, let's go from here," (JOHN 14:31 NASB).

"Peace I leave with you; My peace I give to you; Not as the world gives, do I give to you. Let your heart not be troubled, do not let it be fearful," (JOHN 14:27 NASB).

Ok – I can go on now.

I climbed out of the feathered hideout and continued down the secret path in the uncharted territory.

Thank you, Lord, for the amazing future you have planned for me and that You always stay with me, very near me. Thank You for the joy of just pondering the possibilities of Your mysterious future and knowing You are with me. I will follow You wherever You want me to go. I will give You glory. Continue to show me the steps that You want me to take. I want to be that rainbow in the cloud, helping others find hope and joy in the midst of the storm. I love You.

*"Men ask for a rainbow in the cloud, but I would ask
more from Thee. I would be, in my cloud,
myself a rainbow a minister to other's joy."
(Matheson and Mrs. Charles Cowman)*

✉ Sent: Wednesday, March 27, 2013

✉ Subject: Next Chapter 3-27-13 Easter Hop!!! /Both Numbers Dropped

Yes, call it what you want, but we're doin' a double happy dance!!! Hoppin-all around, like squirrels doin' summersaults. My husband and I actually saw two squirrels showin' us how it's done. It was hilarious!

Bottom line: Both of the main numbers dropped on this last test!!! Thank You Jesus!!!

*Free Light Chain (MM - Multiple Myeloma/blood cancer) now at 70!!!

> Started treatment in October at 557

> Last check 94

> Goal: 15

*Creatinine (Kidney Function) now at 2.37!!!

> Started treatment in October at 2.14

> These counts have been wiggling at 2.5+ for what seems like a very long time.

> Goal: 1.0 with restored/normal kidney function (drink LOTS of water)

Both Dr. Onc and Dr. Kidney agree that once the Myeloma clears out of the kidneys, the kidney numbers should improve even more.

Dr. Onc is very hopeful. Because this has been such a long, slow process. Slow in seeing changes and clearing, that the Myeloma is most likely a slow growing and not so aggressive *dis-ease* in my case. As opposed to a fast responding, fast growing, more aggressive variation. In other words, the tortoise wins the race!

I must say, that given a choice, I would not have chosen this road to walk down. It didn't look like there was any winning this race. However I am seeing so many very positive things in the midst of it. (My Father knew best!!!)

Reorganized priorities

Special times with special people

Little things, formally overlooked, are now treasures

Relationships with people I would not have met

Creativity in how to live

I have all my hair and longer eye lashes than ever!!! Fun (Doc even said I looked like a model. My husband is always saying stuff like that!!!

Even some extra weight to help with the journey, and it's okay!

And I'm in Great Company.

Easter week over 2000 years ago, Jesus had a similar, but much more intense situation. He faced the *dis-ease* of sin and the crucifixion on a cross. However, after agonizing, and pleading, He finally said to His Father,

"Not My will, but Yours be done," (Luke 22:42 NIV).

"Not my way, I'll do it Your way. You know best! (Paraphrase mine.)

And you know, what started out horrible, turned out wonderful. The earth quaked, darkness covered everything, Jesus gave up His life, He was buried, three days later, the stone of the tomb was rolled away, He was alive! And still is. SHINE... Power...LIFE!!!! So many possibilities!

His-story!!!

My example!!!

In Good Hands,

He IS Risen!

Jeri

Sent: Wednesday, April 17, 2013

Subject: Next Chapter 4-17-13 Steady On/Not Much Movement

Hello again!

It's spring. The sun is shining more. The flowers are popping. The birds are singing. There is a sweet fragrance in the air. The sky is constantly being reset with colors and shapes. I love to watch the seasons change. It feels good!!!

I'd like to see my numbers change, but that's a slow process. Steady on!!!

Bottom line: The numbers haven't moved much through Round 9.

Dr. Oncology thinks it could be one of two things:

1. There has been an additional fight going on in my body as I battle an infection, Cellulitis, this time in my little finger. Antibiotics have been prescribed. (It was very strange, swollen, red-streaked, and painful. It's gone now. Thank You, Jesus.)

And/or

2. We may be hitting the *plateau-remission* that he's been waiting for. He's hopeful that the numbers will still drop closer to normal, especially the kidney numbers. NUMBERS DROP!!!!

So we will do at least Round 10 of chemo, which started yesterday. (April 16, 2013)

MM now at 71, last check 70

Creatinine numbers are now at 2.62 last check 2.74. They had been as low as 2.37.

Learning to be patient in a slow season can be a challenge, but I'm learning! I have to be careful not to jump out into the future and all the *what-ifs*. It's just not a good place to go with all the concerns, questions, possibilities, and distractions. If I jump there, I miss what's going on in the day I'm living and there's so much to live in this day.

Sooooo, I continue to practice the *dialect of thanksgiving* and finding people and things around me that I am thankful for: memorable furniture moved into the new spaces, surprise gadgets, magnets, Easter sunrise, clam digging, weeds cleared, flowers coming to life, special chats, meals, cards, texts, emails, ~~haircuts~~, - change that - hair trims because I have hair and want to let it grow, "wallet heroes" who return a money-filled wallet, surprise thank you, Cool Houles under three roofs, hugs, walks, stomping partners, prayers, quiet thoughts, new recipes to try, hummingbird's eye-to-eye greeting, smooth flying, senior shows, proud parent moments, special deliveries...and steady on it goes. Thanks for listening.

Stomping on!

In Good Hands,

Jeri

📧 Sent: Thursday, May 9, 2013

📧 Subject: Next Chapter 5-9-13 Mixed Bag/Partial Remission

Good Morning,

It is a good morning; more sunshine, more flowers, more birds singing, and as a friend said many years ago, "The Lord's still on His Throne."

That's one of my themes this week!!!

Bottom Line: Plateau/Partial Remission

Dr. Onc is referring to this place as a plateau, aka: **partial remission.** The Multiple Myeloma (MM) number has remained in the 70's for the last 3 tests. He has changed the *treatment* (injects/pills/pills) to a *maintenance schedule* (pills), with a follow up every month. He will also be taking my case to the *Lymphoma, Myeloma Conference* where many other specialists will hear the particulars about my odd case.* At the conference they will either be confirming or adjusting the current plans. (May 14).

Dr. Kidney is calling my 2.5-ish Creatinine numbers as my new normal. She said, "You can live with that. Your kidneys are stable; we knew they had a lot of scar-tissue when we started. However, they are not getting any worse and at the improved 40% function you can live **without** dialysis. Keep drinking lots of water!!! Follow up every three months."

This battle is a very strange thing to wrap my head around....

I've taken the medicine, drunk the water, slept, stayed away from people with colds, walked, cried, laughed...and still IT lingers. And even though they say MM will attack again, IT can NOT be my focus. If I am looking around every corner for IT to become active again, I lose THIS day.

I'm not that different from anyone else. I MAY know what MIGHT be coming to challenge my breath and life but I'm still very alive!!! Yes, there were some dark days. Some might say a pit with very dark clouds, but my feet are on a ROCK and the skies are clear!!! I choose to live life today to its fullest. Some things just don't matter; I must let some things go.

And even as I reread this, I must do as I say and pick up the *stomping-dancing shoes* and get on with life!

Be in Good Hands,
Jeri

*Odd case: MM is a slippery *dis-ease*. Each case is very different. My case isn't following the *rules* that are lined out on many of the website and resource information sources. AND researchers are coming up with some amazing new tools (aka: treatments) that are proving to be very effective. But in any case, "God is still on His Throne!"

PS - "What if all you had today is what you thanked God for yesterday?"

The bells on my phone still ring seven times a day, to remind me to be thankful. It is my choice and I ask, "What am I thankful for?"

✉ Sent: Wednesday, May 22, 2013
✉ Subject: Footnote 5-22-13 Footnote/"Good Candidate"

Just a quick note....

Dr. Onc's nurse called last week, just before we left for Ohio-graduation. She informed me that the conference board had reviewed my case and determined I would be a good candidate for a stem cell transplant.

We will meet with the doctor at Oregon Health and Science University* June 11 to discuss risks-benefits. I'll keep you posted.

In Good Hands,
Jeri

*OHSU is a research, education hospital located in Portland, Oregon. Dr. Onc has a partnership with this facility for stem cell transplants. I would be under the care of Dr. OHSU during the procedure if everyone agrees this is the best way to go.

Sent: Friday, May 31, 2013
Subject: Next Chapter 5-31-13 Back Up/Numbers Jump

Wow! It's already the last day of May. The sun came back out!!! There was a robin singing in the tree this morning that answered my whistle, back and forth for about fifteen minutes. I loved it!

He was enjoying his perch, soaking up all the bright light. I'm sure that bird must have been wondering, What?????? But he kept glancing down at me and continued his song. I followed his lead and spent much of the morning in the yard. Enjoying the moment(s).

Some moments are more enjoyable than others....

We had the monthly maintenance-check-up with Dr. Onc this week.

Bottom line: The MM numbers took a jump back up from 70 to 120.7. Disappointed. "I don't like those numbers."

(He thought that this partial remission and maintenance drug would last for years...one month later...)

RATS!!!! That's not what I wanted to hear!

Plan:

> Re-do the labs next week before talking to Dr. OHSU on June 11
>
> Find out where stem cell transplant (SCT) would fit into my treatment, if at all

Probably more chemo to get the best remission possible

Meet with Dr. OHSU

Okay, not what I wanted to hear at all, but a good reminder to live in the moment(s). Today, right now, with what I have in front of me: Baked some muffins, lit a candle, played a silly game on my iPad, took pictures of my front yard flowers, sent a few text messages, ate some sturgeon that we caught in the rain this weekend. A quiet evening at home with college baseball on the radio. Well okay, not so quiet as the Oregon State Beavers squeaked out a win in one game. And I left the room while the University of Oregon Ducks were still on the pond, I mean mound.

The bells ring to remind me to be thankful throughout the day.

Thanks for listening.

I AM in Good Hands - enjoying the moment!!!

Jeri

Sent: Wednesday, June 12, 2013

Subject: Next Chapter 6-11-13 Pivotal Day/Stem Cell Transplant Being Set Up

Good late evening,

I just reread this, lots of words and details...ready? Come back to it later if you want.

It's been one of those pivotal days that I'm sure we'll look back on and remember where we were when we made these decisions and heard the news. My husband and I met with Dr. OHSU this afternoon regarding the possibility of using what is called a Stem Cell Transplant* (SCT) as a tool to fight this crazy, up to this point, non-curable blood cancer; Multiple Myeloma (MM).

Bottom Line: Dr. OHSU says, "You are a good candidate" A mid-July SCT is being set up.

A few qualifying tests need to be run before a mid-July SCT would take place.

> Qualifying tests include:
>
> Updated Bone Marrow Biopsy (ouch)
>
> Updated Skeletal Survey (X-ray)
>
> Heart (echo echo cardio gram gram)
>
> Pulmonary (breathe)

Details:

*When these tests are completed and they are still satisfied that I qualify, the doctors and labs technicians will:

> Harvest *my own stem* cells. There is less chance of rejection.
>
> After two or three days of outpatient "harvesting," "cleaning" and "storing" my stem cells, they admit me to the hospital for a two or three week stay.
>
> Give me a high dose of chemo drugs and basically destroy all the blood in my body. The *good guys* (healthy blood) and the *bad guys* (unhealthy blood) are all destroyed.
>
> Once the MM is punched down into a deep remission, they give me back the stored up stem cells.
>
> This is where my body starts producing new healthy blood.
>
> The team in the hospital keeps a real close eye on all the blood counts and body temperature to help

me fight off infections until my body becomes strong enough to do it on its own.

After discharge, I'm on a pretty *short leash* for a month after I come home.

Trips back to the doc to get checked and begin *maintenance*, etc.

No public outings for six to eight weeks. Some go back to work in three months.

However substitute teaching is not one of those jobs he recommends going back to with all the sniffles and coughs that are in the schools, for at least a year, if then. Hmmmmm!

Goal:

Get the MM into a deep remission. Dr. OHSU says the *average remission* is 4 years before there would need to be a new battle plan. (Without it, the numbers are already trying to come back up.) **But with MM each case is different.** Once you've learned about a MM case, you've learned about ONE case of MM.

It's starting to sound like chocolate...peanut MM's, plain MM's, peanut-butter MM 's, almond MM 's, a whole case of MM 's. They come in all colors and varieties. Melt in your mouth, not in your hand. I bet you could even STOMP on them!!! Thought a commercial break was needed here!!!

It's a lot to face and honestly it doesn't sound like a lot of fun. However, I am feeling like this is the next step in the *uncharted territory* that Jesus is having me walk. And ya know, He hasn't given me the map. So, I'm gonna have to trust Him and lean on the promise that He is always with me, He loves me and will guide me in the ways I should go...and where to stop and rest!!!

He's in control.

I can get out ahead of the plan, try to fix things or go my own way. That *short leash* will come in handy. I get to learn to be a follower, just like training my dogs. We made many pivots and swivels in the street to make sure the dogs knew who was leading and directing, making unexpected turns on a short leash, so they would learn to be followers. Sit...Stay...Down....

Oh soooo many parallels.

Lead on Lord!

Thanks for listening

In Good Hands,

Jeri

Eagles

Eagles soar. They also molt.

Stem Cell Transplant was sounding more like a *molting season.*

Weak,   Soar.

Tired,   Life,

Bald,   Restored,

Isolated,   Strengthened,

Near death...

I took courage in the fact that even though the eagle is down, weak and helpless for a time, eventually the majestic bird is renewed and strengthened and returns to the skies to soar again.

As the possibility of a Stem Cell Transplant was becoming a reality, I was troubled. I went back and forth between thinking this was a good plan and then going through memories of watching my Mom go through two Stem Cell Transplants while battling the Multiple Myeloma. She made the best of it, but she was weak, tired, "puffy" with extra fluids, near death, bald, isolated, nauseated, had mouth sores, and was hooked up to IV's. Then in recovery she slowly climbed back to a stable condition in a hotel room near the hospital for a month, then home *under quarantine.* Eventually, she did return to *new normal* life for

— 101 —

almost ten years, before she couldn't fight anymore. It was NOT fun to watch and really NOT fun thinking about doing the same thing.

I felt like, physically, everything was going to fall apart. I would be molting, BUT:

> ...Those who WAIT for the Lord will gain new strength; they will mount up with wings as eagles...(ISAIAH 40:31 NASB).

Renew their strength...their strength was gone...but it returned...a story of hope.

If the eagle can do it, so can I.

Help me be brave, Jesus!

Sweet
Summer
Days!

Mt. Hood / Lost Lake

Vertical Trampoline!

Backyard Therapy!

Changed Forever!

Warm Summer Nights!

Bee Still!

SECTION 5: SUMMER 2013

Got It Back

Make Every Day Count

I had accepted the fact that the Stem Cell Transplant required a hospital stay, and that quarantined living arrangements would be the highlight for my summer. However when Dr. OHSU announced that he wanted to put the transplant on hold, summer got a whole lot brighter. The excitement was comparable to being asked if I wanted to float through the Grand Canyon. We walked out of the doctor's office into the possibilities of making plans for the summer and fall. Make every day count.

✉ Sent: Friday, June 28, 2013

✉ Subject: Next Chapter June 29, 2013 Closed Doors/Transplant On Hold

Oh Happy Day!

Surprise, the hospital doors are shut and summer has been given back!!!

Somehow the flowers smell sweeter, Mt. Hood looks more majestic, the baby birds come into view and the sun seems warmer. And it really is warmer with record highs in the forecast. I love it!

Bottom line: The stem cell transplant has been put on hold!

I passed all of the tests that were required.

We attended an orientation class and received a two-inch notebook of information to wade through. Wow...

Started cleaning, scrubbing, disinfecting our house, etc. We were getting ready.

HOWEVER, MM (Multiple Myeloma) doesn't follow any rules.

During the required *rest-wait period* from the last *treatment medicines*, the Light Chain Counts (MM) went from 70, a partial remission, and jumped to 120 and then jumped again to 223. BAD TREND!!!

We saw Dr. OHSU today. He wasn't happy with the aggressive growth of this *dis-ease*.

Next plan:

>Begin new chemo treatment July 12 (28 day cycles - 1x/week injection/pills)
>
>MM numbers <100 (might take 3 or 4 cycles)
>
>Revisit the Stem Cell Transplant idea
>
>Continue watching the kidneys improve!!!!!!

Yes, there is still a battle to be fought, but today is a celebration day and I am reminded again to enjoy each moment in the moment. I am thankful for a cleaner house, garage sale plans, special dinners AND dessert, weeded yards, sunny days, forest drives, cards, notes, emails, phone calls, silly games, movies, recorded TV that can skip commercials, baby birds, butterflies, prayers, encouraging words, quality of life, improving kidneys, bike rides, hair/eyelashes, blueberries, strawberries, memorable pictures and sunsets at the coast. I practice finding the good things in days like this, so that the *harder* days aren't so hard.

Thanks for stomping.

In Good Hands,

Jeri

Full Circle

With the transplant on hold and the river of life in a floating pattern, there was some breathing room, time to reflect. I knew there was another set of rapids and more wild rides ahead, but it was time for some thinking, hiking, and stretching my legs.

On our Grand Canyon adventure we took hikes that led away from the river. However, there was always an option to stay back with the raft. The hikers went out on what seemed like uncharted trails and found treasures in the wilderness. But we always made it back, full circle, to the river.

At this point in my writing, the story wanders from the cancer battle and into the uncharted trail tracing through the life of loved ones who have died. I will eventually make it back, full circle, back to the story. Reader, I invite you to come along on the hike. If, however, you would like to stay with the current story, skip ahead to the next section titled *Be Still.*

In the years leading up to the cancer diagnosis, there were many experiences in the *good hard lessons* of loved ones dying and then adjusting to major shifts in the family dynamics that taught precious life lessons. Life really does go full circle. These difficult times uncovered pain, loss, and suffering and at the same time revealed joy, peace and hope. I was learning all along. It is a process!

And in the process of living life through the good and the hard, I realized the Lord really had been preparing me for what was coming next in my own life. When my world was rocked with the cancer diagnosis, I had NOT thought about all these precious people and the *shifts to my normal* when they died. However, looking back, my heart really was full of treasured nuggets of *hope* that helped me navigate my own journey towards living a full circle of life. As the gates of heaven draw closer and I face the reality of immortality, there are treasures to find; nuggets that add to my heart.

This is the *short list* of the nuggets. The stories that follow will give their origins.

- Heaven is a real place.
- We're gonna make it.
- Loss hurts! Even four-legged loss. Grief is a process.
- We honored her request for privacy.
- I was there.
- Get close, even if it is hard.
- Determined to at least knock.
- "She's not here, she's in heaven."
- When we love much, we grieve much…love anyway.
- People often need reassurance to "let go."
- So, do not worry! My Heavenly Father knows my need.
- I will trust you Lord, no matter what You decide.
- Life WILL go on.
- Once reassured, he relaxed.
- She didn't recognize me. But, I'm glad I was there.
- "Her dead body looks nothing like the future, resurrected, blooming life she will know in heaven."
- "We're-gonna-make-it!"
- "Cancer may take years from my life, but it will not take life

from my years!"

- Some people actually wait to be alone before letting go.
- God gives what is needed for each situation.
- I am not alone!
- "The Good Lord won't give me any more than I can handle."
- Share sweet memories and stories of her life.
- She must have known it was time.
- "We knew this was coming."
- It's ok to be mad.
- Keep Watching!

The **nuggets of life** lessons are in bold letters within the stories on the next few pages. These loved ones have helped to shape my life. They have lived and died and returned to our Maker; they have gone *Full Circle*. And they have deposited much more into my life than I can put to words.

Six years before I was born, in the summer of 1956, my uncle, Mom's brother, died in Alaska. The young adult had been missing for days when rescuers found his body in an icy river after his solo hiking adventure went terribly wrong. I can't imagine the grief Mom and my grandparents went through at that time. However, when I was about eight years old, I was really mad at God for taking my uncle away before I even got to meet him. I cried. For days, I cried. Mom said he was in heaven. And if I had faith, I would see him one day, but not now.

"What is faith?"

"Believing in something you don't see or understand, but trust that it's real. God's taking care of him. You can't see him now. You must let him go."

Ok, so heaven has my uncle and God is taking care of him. I could let him go. It was done. This is my first connection to death. **Heaven is a real place.**

One of the most devastating losses came with the death of my family. In the summer of 1966, the divorce was final. I was four years old. My brother and I lived with Mom. Dad didn't live with us anymore. I remember sobbing, hoping that my parents would get back together. I didn't understand all the *adult things* that were going on. My dreams were dashed when Dad said he was going to remarry. What a confusing time. My world was shattered. I was numb. I tried to cover up my grief with a smiley face. This wasn't something that was going to go away or get fixed. However, I do remember Mom saying, **"We're gonna make it."** She said that a lot. We all needed to hear those words and adopt that attitude. I can look back now and know for sure that Mom and Dad did the best they could, given the choices that were made. They BOTH really did love me. And my heavenly Father was there all the time.

Grief came calling one evening when I was about nine years old with a knock on the door. Mom returned to the table in tears and said our little dog had been hit by a car and killed. Oh ouch! I was devastated. My heart hurt. Mom wrote a sealed note to my 4th grade teacher, I'm sure explaining my red eyes and weepy disposition.

Loss hurts! Even four-legged loss. Grief is a process.

In the summer of 1975 Mom got remarried. Pop, my stepfather, and I have a good relationship now. But we didn't start out on a good foot. He came into our lives as I was entering junior high. At the time, I felt like he was taking Mom away. However, I can see now that he provided for our family in ways that I didn't appreciate in those days. He tried. I didn't make it easy for him. I needed some life experiences of my own to fully appreciate what a gift he is to me.

In the summer of 1977, our childhood babysitter entered the gates of heaven behind closed doors. She didn't want visitors, including my brother or me, to see her weakening, cancer-filled body. It saddened me, but we honored her request.

I loved her hand-mixed chocolate chip cookies. She included me in the frequent tea parties that were held with Mom when she came to pick us up. I loved being with them. One day, our babysitter asked my brother and me whose birthday was on December 25. She had us guessing for a long time before she finally told us – "Jesus"! I'll never forget. (When I got to be older, and had my own kids, we had Birthday parties to celebrate Jesus' birthday.) Her frustration/cuss word was "Oh, sugar!" We always knew when it was cleaning day; Pine-sol filled the air. I didn't realize it at the time, but our babysitter had rescued our single-parent, two-kids family with her warm, open hospitality. She became like a second mom to us, which allowed my Mom some flexibility to work and provide for our little trio family. I am grateful. At the end of her life, I wonder if staying away was the right thing. But we **honored her request for privacy.**

Three years later, in the spring of 1980, my uncle, my Dad's brother, was killed in a snowmobiling accident. The mountain of snow crushed him in an avalanche. He was a husband and father of three girls. As a senior in high school and emotionally distant from my uncle, I was numb. I witnessed the grief on the other family members. Again I couldn't imagine the grief my Dad, Aunt, Cousins, and Grandparents were experiencing. The only thing I knew to do was run after my baby cousin, which gave her grieving mom some space. God had me on assignment. **I was there.**

A year and a half later, on Christmas Eve, 1981, Grandpa, my Mom's Dad, entered the gates of heaven after a battle with prostrate/lung cancer. He had been my fishing instructor, hiking scout, pocketknife teacher, and "first boyfriend." He would often say, "Penny for your thoughts" when asking for an in-depth conversation.

On my last earthly visit with him, Grandpa had been reduced from a strong, burly, independent teddy bear to a frail, hunched-over, needy wisp of a man. By the end of my two-week Arizona visit, he spent more time lying in bed than up. One night I sat beside his bed and he looked into my eyes. For the first time in my life, I saw my Grandpa cry. I cried, too. He told me he was really glad I was there and showed me it was important to **get close—even if it is hard**. To tell you the truth, I wanted to run.

He also said maybe someday I would help someone who was sick and dying, so it was good that I saw him like this. He said he loved me, gave me a hug, full of meaning, and insisted that I return to college in Oregon.

Mom and I crossed mid-air as she came to help my Grandma with his care. Grandpa entered an assisted care facility and walked to the gates from there. He gave me a peek at the deterioration of the physical body and taught me not to be afraid of it. Even though I wanted to run, it was really hard to return to school. I can see now I wasn't ready for the journey…yet! But I missed not being there.

___

Life continued on. I graduated from college. I was married. I found a teaching job in the public schools.

Two years later, in the fall of 1987, my co-kindergarten teacher went home to be with Jesus. This teacher was an English lady who helped me navigate my second public school teaching assignment. She was a tremendous help and encouragement. As we worked and shared, we became more than teaching buddies; we became friends. She had shared that she was a cancer survivor. After working together for a few years she retired, only to discover the cancer had returned. She closed the doors to visitors. However, I was **determined to at least knock**. The door opened a crack. I was privileged to spend a few moments with her. She was curled up on her couch, her body wasting away, but her spirit was bright. We shared a few laughs and some tears. Heaven's gates opened up for her a few weeks later. I'm glad I knocked.

___

By 1991, we had two beautiful children.

In 1995, I started a new job at the church we were attending. I was a children's pastor.

Three years passed and in the early spring of 1998, my husband's grandma entered the gates of heaven. I only knew this precious, redheaded lady for a few years, but she was special. Grandma lived in La Grande. The year I lived and worked in Joseph was a year of traveling back and forth to see my future husband in Beaverton. I would often arrange to swing by her house and pick her up for the hour-long drive to Pendleton. She would visit my future in-laws for the weekend. I would pick her up again on my way back through and take her home. She had a delightful laugh and we had many sweet conversations. Age took its toll.

A few years after meeting her, our little family was escorted to the front row of her open casket service. That was the closest I had ever been to a "shell of a person." It was a bit shocking for us all.

"She's not here, she's in heaven."

Over the years, the Cool Houle family pets have given us all teachable moments about enjoying life and also experiencing death. Bailey, Mac, Doc, Freckles, and Mango were all dearly loved and deeply missed. We discovered a full spectrum of emotions: a capacity to feel deep and know we are very much alive...especially with a wet, sloppy kiss from a happy, tail-wagging friend. **When we love much, we grieve much...love anyway.**

Three years later, in the early spring of 2001, my Dad's Dad, entered into the gates of heaven. Grandpa's body shut down from complications of a hiatal hernia. He was a private man, at least with me. We didn't share many words. But Grandpa loved flowers. He planted large plots of dahlias, marigolds, and zinnias in front of their little farm home and planted iris down the long driveway. A very inviting gesture.

He always welcomed me into his life. When I was a very little girl, Grandpa invited me to a horse show to help him hand out winning ribbons to the riders. My little cowgirl outfit and go-go boots were his idea. I still remember the *clicky* sound that those boots made on the floor. I loved it!

Grandpa played solitaire with a deck of cards on a large lapboard across his Lazy Boy chair. His crutches leaned close by. He didn't let a hip injury stop him from living life. He shared his homemade fruitcakes and peanut brittle at Christmas and apples and fish in the summer and fall.

On Grandpa's final day here on earth, he lay in a hospital bed, with eyes closed and breath shallow. As I arrived, my Dad was in the hallway, having said his goodbyes, and Grandma was weeping beside Grandpa. I remember learning that in the process of dying, **people often need reassurance to "let go."** I hugged my Grandma, squeezed my Grandpa's hand and told him I loved him. I also told him I would help make sure Grandma was okay and that he could go to heaven with Jesus. Peace came into the room and within a few more labored breaths he was gone from us. The nurse confirmed it.

I spent the week in Corvallis with my Grandma and Dad, discovering the amazing amount of preparation Grandpa had done before he "changed his address." I watched my Dad, with his spiral notebook, carry out executor duties, finalizing Grandpa's earthly life.

At the funeral home, when the director asked about church affiliation and who would officiate the service, both my Dad and my Grandma looked at me. I was their church affiliation. Inside I was screaming…"NO!" But out of my mouth came…"I can do that."

Oh, Jesus help!!!

After connecting with a pastor friend that lived in town and hours of prayer and study, the creative service came together.

Thank you, Jesus!!!

With a helium balloon and a tack, I described how Grandpa

had been full of life, then "pop," a limp balloon/body. His spirit, like the helium, was rising heavenward.

This scripture became very real to me during the week.

> **Therefore I tell you, do not worry about your life, what you will eat or drink; or about your body what you will wear...** (MATTHEW 6:25-34 NIV).

When I received the call that Grandpa was getting ready to leave earth, I packed a few things and drove towards the hospital, not sure if I would make it in time to say so-long; I made it within minutes of his departure.

Dad made sure we all were eating. And when the day of the service arrived, my sweats and jeans just wouldn't cut it. Dad found a dress shop in town and clothed me!

> **So, do not worry... My Heavenly Father knows (my need.) But seek first His kingdom and His righteousness and all these things will be given to you as well. (So,) do not worry about tomorrow for tomorrow will worry about itself. Each day has enough trouble of its own**
> (MATTHEW 6:31-34 NIV paraphrase mine).

Two and a half years passed and in the winter of 2003, my friend and co-worker walked through the gates of heaven. Within six months from retiring from her job, cancer invaded her body.

My friend was a very caring, praying, loving lady. She helped many people see themselves the way God sees them, wanting them free. She believed God would heal her from the aggressive cancer that was taking away her life. She asked a group of friends to stand and believe with her for healing. And when she could no longer stand we carried her, sometimes literally, and in prayer.

Besides praying, I didn't know what I would do. I knocked on the door. It was open to me. Some days my friend was awake, some days she was not. Sometimes we would talk, then cry, then laugh and pray. I sang over her. She especially wanted her son to know Jesus. I promised her I would continue to pray for him. Sometimes I did the dishes or played cards with her grown kids in the room where she rested. She told us later, she enjoyed hearing our laughter.

As her physical body was giving up, she asked the prayer team/friends to continue to pray for her healing, even after her death. She hoped to be healed and awaken from death.

I will trust you Lord – no matter what you decide.

She died, we prayed four days, just like Lazarus in the Bible. We all believed she would be healed. She was…just not like we thought.

God, Your will, not mine.

As I think about it now, why would anyone, after seeing the face of Jesus and experiencing the love and beauty of heaven, ever want to return to this earth.

We released her. However, this death, the death of a close friend…rocked my world.

Death of a loved one is like having the house hit by a tornado. Nothing is in its rightful place. In time, things and emotions return to some kind of order. I've been told it's healthy to have one room that is left closed: a grieving room. Come and go, in and out of the room, but don't live there. Give myself permission to grieve. Eventually, even that room will become ordered, too.

Life WILL go on.

Two years later, in the fall of 2005, my husband's dad walked through the gates of heaven. He was husband, dad to his own family, and uncle to many. He accepted me with a look in his eye and openness in his heart. I truly felt like I belonged in this new family. He had a contagious laugh and a love of pie and fishing that he has passed down to many of the sons and "daughters" in his family line.

As the lung cancer advanced and he drew nearer to death, his sons, their wives and families drew nearer to him and his wife, my mother-in-law. We shared memories, joys, tears… and many meals.

When my father-in-law was no longer able to care for himself and his needs became more than any of us could manage, he was moved to a care center just down the street from the family home.

One day, as my husband was reading the Bible to his dad, his dad spoke up and asked,

"Am I a good fish or a bad fish?"

"Oh, Dad, you are a good fish. You're a keeper."

Once reassured, he relaxed.

On another occasion, all five boys were gathered around his bed. (I was the mouse in the corner!) He spoke to each of his sons. Precious!

I was honored when he asked one of his sons and me to co-officiate the service. The brothers asked me to speak about the hope of heaven. The creative message included a clay strawberry pot with holes, representing the broken body and a lit candle. In life, the candle is lit on the inside with the Light of Jesus. In death, the candle is still lit, but now lit in heaven, outside the body, in good standing.

Also in the fall of 2005, my husband's grandma slipped into the gates of heaven while we were caring for his dad. She went without anyone knowing she was even headed that way. She was a spunky lady who lived alone in her own home. She was always ready to feed us and dodged the camera with finesse. Maybe she didn't want too much attention. Another Rose for heaven.

Six months later, in the spring of 2006, my Dad's mom, joined her life-long buddy on the other side of the gates. It was exactly five years, to the day, of Grandpa's exit. Just like Grandpa, Grandma was known for her flowers, especially the rows of spring daffodils. Also, she was known for the pies. Even though she had baked thousand's of them in her job as a baker, she loved to bake for her family. Grandma was very playful, too.

When we were little she played the tag game, "The Fox and the Eggs," with my brother and me. We would run, chasing the "fox" around the house for the "colored egg"! I'm not sure how we kept up with her. We all slept real well after that.

I remember her holding my hands and saying, "You have such pretty hands and long eyelashes." During a holiday season or a birthday we would each receive a Hallmark card in the mail with a $2 bill slipped inside.

As she neared death, **she didn't recognize me. But, I'm glad I was there.** Alzheimer's had stolen her memory and her body was shutting down. She slipped into a coma. On my last visit, with harp music in the background and Dad reading quietly in the corner, I leaned over to Grandma and whispered to her.

"I love you, Grandma. It's okay to go home to be with Jesus. I will see you in heaven some day."

I left her that day knowing it would be the last time I would see her on this side of heaven. By the time I had driven home, my Dad called and said she had died. Grandma had slipped peacefully through the gates of heaven.

Once again, Dad asked if I would officiate the service.

"Oh Jesus, please help!!!"

In this creative service, there was a daffodil bulb and an actual blooming daffodil flower. I compared the dead-looking bulb with the blooming flower; the bulb looks nothing like the flower. Just like Grandma's dead body looks nothing like the future, resurrected blooming life she will know in heaven.

"Thank You, Jesus!"

Whew!

This "hike" just keeps on going. Doing okay, Reader?

Let's stop for a short break.

In the Grand Canyon, when the long, hot hike got to be too much, we stopped and caught our breath, let our aching muscles rest, and drank lots of water. One particular hike went straight up the side of the canyon and, of course, straight down. We didn't think it would ever end. Our guide correctly described this hike as, "The Stairmaster from H***"! I must say, however, it was worth the climb.

In next phase of the *Full Circle* "hike," I can tell you, I was much more involved in my loved one's journey to the gates of heaven. And when the "long, hot hike" got to be too much, I stopped and took a deep breath, allowed my aching heart to cry and drank lots of water. I will admit, there were moments when I wondered how long the struggle would go on. But, it was definitely worth the "climb".

Let's go on...

Six months later, in the winter of 2006, my mom, was promoted to heaven one day before her birthday. She finished her year here and started her next one in heaven. There are books that could be written about my persevering, patient, encouraging Mom. Even when my brother and I were little, she had this **we're-gonna-make-it** attitude. As a single parent, I believe she said that to encourage herself as well as my brother and me. In those days, we lived paycheck to paycheck. But we were happy: pizza after payday, walks to the park, summer swim passes, puppies, healthy meals, warm cookies, road trips, patience, love.

Mom loved to sew and cook. In her 10-year battle with Multiple Myeloma, she used her sewing skills to create amazing quilts. One quilt, she called her *Covering*, was stitched with some of her favorite things: teapots, teacups, chocolate, butterflies, quotes, scriptures, purples and pinks. She took this *Covering* to treatments and hospital visits to remind herself that God was her *Covering*. She also shared her gift of cooking. She hosted many, many tea parties.

The *dis-ease* stole more and more of her energy. However, cheerfully she would say, "I might not be able to <a,b,c> but I can still <x,y,z>." I still find little notes she wrote telling me how much she loved me. Traveling was one thing on her "life list." She and Pop went on many adventures between her doctor appointments, treatments and blood transfusions. They traveled the world. She lived life to the fullest, living out the motto she had adopted:

"Cancer may take years from my life, but it will not take life from my years!"

In the final days at the hospital, the doctor said she would not come out of these woods. He was right. I cried; we all cried. We all loved her so much and she loved us. She had so many things she still wanted to do. One of the nurses reminded her of how many things she had done. She didn't want to give up. Her body just couldn't keep up. She fought a good fight!

"I'm gonna miss you so much, Mom."

I really didn't want her to leave so soon. But I had to release her. In our final farewell conversation, my husband and I encouraged her to set up another tea party at the Banqueting Table in heaven and to save us a chair.

"I love you, Mom. It's okay to go."

She opened one eye as we left the room and slipped away through the gates shortly after that. I was told, later, that some people actually wait to be alone before letting go of this world. So, in the privacy of her own timing, she let go. She will always be "My Hero!"

———————

Pop, my stepdad, and I shared many tearful moments and deep breaths after Mom died. He and I continue to touch base. He has been extremely helpful and encouraging to me in my own battle with MM, and a source of reassurance to both my husband and me. He's walked this road before us. And I still have much to learn from him. He will always be one of the "Knights" in my life.

———————

That was a really, really tough time. It seemed like death just kept knocking on our door and taking loved ones away. We hardly had time to process one major loss and there was another and another. The loss seemed to be cutting deeper and deeper. I was reminded to "give myself permission to grieve."

"You never really get over the loss, you just learn to live with it."

"Jesus will carry you."

"It's okay to be at 75%."

"With time you'll be able to put the grief card in your pocket, take it out, look at it now and then…then put it away. You'll know it's there, but you don't have to stare at it all the time."

God gives what is needed for each situation.

GRACE. When I think about walking with someone to the gates of heaven, it's overwhelming. I never know, going into it, what I'm going to do. All I know is: I want to be there, be close, and love. I pray that Jesus shows me how. These are special assignments. I must trust Jesus and release my loved ones into His care. It's a "good-hard privilege."

_____

In the spring of 2007 our son graduated from High School. He left home within a month for a six-month, semi-local college experience.

In the late fall of 2008 I resigned from my assignment at our church after working there for thirteen years. I was tired, grieving, and making poor decisions. I came home to take care of my family and myself.

In the spring of 2009 our daughter graduated from High School and she left home within a couple of months for a four-year, across the country college experience.

We raised our children to be capable, independent, contributing adults. All along we released them into the Hands of the Lord. Yet having them leave the nest is a whole new process.

Fifteen months later, in the early fall of 2010 my grandma's health began to fail. With Mom gone, Grandma's care was now my "charge." I had visited this independent, maverick, persevering woman many times in her Arizona home, as the caregiver. But as children, my brother and I had spent many summers with Grandma and Grandpa in their Oregon home. We played in the sprinklers, chased butterflies in the yard, ran though the cornrows, and ate carrots with "tails" just like Bugs Bunny. Camping trips were a highlight of our summers.

Grandma loved her garden and her flowers. She was also an excellent cook and seamstress. She enjoyed embroidery, crocheting and knitting, even when her arthritic hands bothered her. There wasn't much she hadn't done. She outlived both her children and three husbands. So, as she aged, I had the privilege of loving her as granddaughter but I also had the privilege of walking with and helping her with her final earthly decisions.

Because I still lived in Oregon and she was in Arizona we often talked on the phone. She would always tell me about her garden, what the temperature was for the day and how her cats were doing. She also let me know about her health and expressed the challenges of living alone. Grandma knew she would eventually need some extra help, but moving back to Oregon or to an assisted living situation "was out"! The southern climate helped bring relief to her arthritic joints and pain riddled back. Grandma and Grandpa had moved to their warmer home years ago and she wasn't budging. She would always say, **"The Good Lord won't give me any more than I can handle."** Then pressed on with His help.

However, after a fall in her garden that broke her hip, she was placed in a rehab center. The social worker met with me and helped navigate this season with Grandma. We both agreed, at 94, she shouldn't live alone anymore. Over time and with some heart felt discussions, Grandma agreed. She moved down the hall to *Assisted Living*.

A few months later, a nurse called to tell me Grandma had a stroke and was sent to the hospital. Before I could get there, she slipped into a coma.

Back in Oregon, I arranged to fly to Arizona to be with her. As I waited for my plane for what would be my last trip to Arizona, doubts and fears were filling my mind. I needed reassurance that I could "be there" for Grandma during this time. A friend called me just before I boarded the plane and thanked me for helping him during a difficult time years earlier. That timely call was very reassuring.

The plane was packed; I had a window seat. The plane had reached cruising altitude. I glanced out the window, wondering…

Jesus, are you with me?

I'm all alone.

Will I get to my Grandma before she dies?

What I saw out the window made me do a double take. There were rainbows, lots of them, on top of the clouds and in circles. It looked like a bowl of Fruit-Loops cereal in a pool of milk. It was spectacular. What a sign from the Lord. I wasn't alone! He was with me!

Thank You, Jesus!

The plane landed in Las Vegas and the black, Texas-plated, PT Cruiser rental car was gassed and ready to drive the two hour trip to Grandma. A speed zone change didn't catch my eye in the O'dark hours of the late night, but my speed caught the eye of the police officer.

"License and registration, please!"

"I'm an Oregon driver, in a Texas-plated rental car, driving in Arizona on my way to the hospital. Hopefully getting there before my Grandma dies."

Handing back my license and rental papers, he said, "Drive safely!"

Thank You, Jesus!

I was on my way again.

When I found Grandma at the hospital, she was unresponsive. Her sweet nurse believed people shouldn't be alone as they die, and she was prepared to stay with her all night. I decided to check into my hotel, but wasn't sure about leaving Grandma all night. So I sent up a *fleece* to the Lord.

"If the hotel has chocolate chip cookies at the front desk hospitality tray, I would stay there."

No cookies anywhere! Dropping off my bags, I headed back to Grandma at the hospital.

No change with Grandma; however, I found out the nurse caring for her was a Christian and offered to call her pastor. So, at 12:30 AM, the three of us stood around my resting Grandma **sharing sweet memories and stories of her life.** I held her hand and laughed and cried. They say the sense of hearing is the last sense to go. She must have been enjoying our chatter because she squeezed my hand and her feet were dancing in the bed, her eyes still closed. The pastor prayed for Grandma (and me) and then left.

I caught a few winks on the couch in the hospital. In the morning, the doctor greeted me.

"We should move her to Hospice in another wing, but let's keep her right here. She doesn't have long."

He turned to the nurse and told her to put together a hospitality cart. Guess what was on that cart? Yep, chocolate chip cookies, Chips Ahoy! And all kinds of drinks, chips, and fruit! Wow!

What comfort!

I left the hospital for a few hours to take care of some business for Grandma. When I returned, the hospitality cart had been refreshed with kitchen baked chocolate chip cookies! What comfort, a small sign **I was not alone.**

Thank You, Jesus.

Grandma was getting weaker. I shared my comfort cookie story with the nurses and then said,

> "The only thing that could make it better is if these cookies were warm and I had a cold glass of milk." (I hadn't eaten any of them...yet!)

> "I'll be right back."

You guessed it. She returned with warm cookies and cold milk. It was such a comfort to me!

Thank You, Jesus.

I know You are here.

Both nurses left for a moment. I stroked Grandma's hair and said,

> "I love you. It's okay to leave. Heaven will be glorious."

As the nurses came back, my cookies and milk gone, we sang some songs over her. There was Peace. The monitors flat lined. She stopped breathing and was gone. One of the nurses said, "Wow! I've never seen anything like that before."

Farewell Grandma.

Thank You, Jesus, my Comfort and Peace.

Only six months passed and in the early spring of 2011, my husbands mom walked through the gates of heaven. This amazing wife and mom of five boys, was delighted with the daughters she gained as her boys married.

She shared many stories with me as a daughter of divorce. We had a lot in common. It was comforting to have an older woman to talk to that understood. I started to see both my Mom and Dad's situation differently.

My mother-in-law had lived alone five and a half years after her husband died. She was suffering from Alzheimer's and cancer. She was moved into a special caregiving home with a private room. She loved seeing her family and repeating her stories. "It was so special!"

We didn't know it would be our last visit at the time, but as my husband and I left her, she said,

"Next time are ya gonna bring the shovel?"

We were puzzled at first. We gave her hugs, said we loved her. **She must have known it was time.** Within the week she slipped through the gates of heaven. The "shovel" was for the graveside service. Gotcha covered. Take care, special lady.

Within days, our son had his right eye removed. The family gathered in the hospital waiting room. Celebrating the life of my mother-in-law and praying for the health and healing of our boy. Our daughter was 2000 miles away, in school, learning her own set of life lessons.

Death wasn't letting up. Six months after that, in the early fall of 2011, my dad passed through the gates of heaven after a

twenty-plus-year battle with cancer.

Dad and I had crisscrossed through each other's lives over the years after the divorce. Both of us missed out on many opportunities. However, on Dad's visits he would take us on adventures! It might be a museum, bookstore, hobby store, airplane ride, college campus exploration, or back to the three-story home for a "weekend-day visit with Dad."

Dad loved his airplanes and electronics, bike riding and healthy eating. Above all, he loved his John Deere tractors.

However, cancer took more and more of his life and energy. Dad and my stepmom decided that he would spend his final days at home. They brought in a hospital bed and set up Hospice Care. He would soon need 24-hour care.

I wanted to be close. I asked if I could come lend a hand and the door opened. I had the privilege of living in their home for his last thirty-seven days. Every day we discovered what the new normal looked like. The physical limitations became very frustrating for the once "Cycle-Oregon-older–athlete." When biking, and then walking wasn't an option, we went for a stroll in the wheel chair.

Before becoming too sick to walk, Dad used to walk to the local Starbucks and have coffee with the "old goats." On the way there, he passed by "The Bush;" a Cotoneaster plant, always noticing its growth pattern: a stick in winter, leaf buds in spring, and little green berries in summer. By the time he and I were strolling by, "The Bush" had pea-sized green berries and shiny green leaves. With the daily bush visit, we began noticing that the berries were changing, turning a bit yellow, then a tinge of orange. Dad called it "God's Bush."

It reminded me of Moses from the Old Testament Bible story where God spoke from a burning bush.

So I asked him, "If it is God's Bush, what do you think He would say to you?"

Dad thought for a while, took the branch that hung over the

sidewalk in his hands and touched a few leaves.

"Keep watching!" he said, his words full of meaning.

He wasn't talking much at this point. The Bush became the destination goal even if we didn't get any further. We got to The Bush.

"Keep watching!" "Keep watching!" "Keep watching!"

One day, after talking about heaven and dying, I asked him another question.

"Do you think the berries will turn red...so you can see them before you go through the gates?"

"Keep watching!"

On the days when Dad felt up to it, we continued strolling on the neighborhood streets, often ending up on a bus route. As the buses went by, I would ask...

"Where do you want to go today, Dad?"

He would always have a different destination:

"Downtown." "The beach." "Ohio."

"What would you do in Ohio?"

"See my granddaughter." (My daughter – away at college)

"San Diego." "Waterfront." "San Francisco." "Grocery store."

"What would you get at the grocery store?"

"Hershey Bar."

"Dark Chocolate or milk chocolate?"

"Milk."

"Nuts or no nuts?"

"No nuts."

We actually had one of the caregivers pick up some Hershey Bars at the store and he enjoyed the chocolate to the end.

We found treasures in this storm during our stroll, little things that mattered:

An orange and black feather, which, as OSU alum, he proudly stuck in his hat,

Squirrels on the wire,

City chickens chasing grapes,

Planes overhead which always put a pause in the stroll as Dad identified the aircraft,

Ducati (European motorcycle) for sale safely displayed in a neighbor's front window,

Firemen on the scene of a burning tree/power line,

Flashlights and hand cranks in the power outage,

Elm tree extraction process,

Painters recoloring houses,

Yard renovations,

Familiar kitties,

Concrete driveways setting up,

The Bush – of course.

There were things to watch. Good distractions. Treasures.

There were also treasured conversations and good, hard times together.

After a 20-plus-year battle with cancer, whenever anyone said something like "I'm so sorry."

Dad would respond, **"We knew this was coming."**

He was ready to die.

At one point I said, "I'm excited for you, Dad. God has a Big House with lots of rooms and a banqueting table. There'll be no more pain or tears. We'll be together again."

He invited me to "hear" his prayers every night and also recited the twenty-third Psalm from memory.

He allowed me to ask some tough questions regarding what happened between Mom and him. There was closure and understanding on lots of levels. We talked through forgiveness for the divorce and for leaving his family. He released the guilt he had carried for years!!! We talked through acceptance, especially God accepting him and his prayers

One day, when Dad was anxious and restless, he said, "I'm tense...intense!!!" (In tents) I said, "No Dad, you're in the house!" He chuckled. We went for a stroll. That night, after the power went out from a fire in the electrical line outside, we talked through his fears about fire and darkness. Eventually Peace came as he realized there was nothing he could do but trust Jesus to protect him.

On another day, we talked through anger using Playdough.

"It's ok to be mad." "I get mad and cry, you get mad and shake the bars on your hospital bed. If we don't let the emotions out, we'll explode or our emotions will come out sideways."

We actually made a purple Playdough man and role-played our emotions. There was a little green ball of anger we put in his stomach that grew bigger and bigger as if the emotions got trapped.

"It's ok to have emotions."

So, we practiced getting mad. I went first.

"I am so mad. Cancer took my Mom away from me and now it's taking my Dad..."

<tears>

And then calm,

"Will you please hand me a Kleenex?"

Then it was Dad's turn.

"I am mad I can't sleep through the night."

<shaking the bars>

Peace.

The Hospice nurse was very reassuring. On one visit, the nurse told Dad he could "break his rules" and eat what he wanted, how much he wanted, whenever he wanted, even if it was chocolate. And if he didn't want to eat, he didn't need to because his body didn't need so much any more.

After she left Dad said, "I really am dying."

"Yes, you are. Your body has done what it needs to do to be ready to leave this earth and go to heaven."

Dad was relieved, "It's peaceful."

On his last evening here on earth a good friend stopped by and asked to see Dad. Dad's face lit up.

"You've fought a good fight." And he prayed, "Jesus scoop him up and take him to heaven with you."

More peace!

Later that same night, at bedtime, knowing the gates were close, Dad said,

"Thank you, Jeri," heavy with meaning.

I repeated the words I had heard earlier:

"You've fought a good fight, Dad."

<Tears>

"Thank you for the privilege of living here with you. I'm going to miss you."

<Tears>

He tenderly stroked my face.

<Tears>

I often asked Dad "what else can I get you" and he would name a simple request. On this last night,

"What else can I get you, Dad?"

"There's nothing more."

And he was right.

The next morning our nighttime caregiver came up the stairs as I was coming down. "Come with me! Hurry!"

He was already through the gates of heaven when I got to the bed…private man.

Before returning to my home that day, I walked to "The Bush." My brother had been on the last few strolls with Dad so I hadn't seen it for a few days…the berries were red!!!

Keep Watching!

———————————

Dad's wife, my stepmother, accepted me into her home during the difficult final days of Dad's life. We shared some of the tough times. I am forever grateful for that opportunity. That time allowed Dad and me to recover many lost pieces in our relationship.

We spend more time together now than we did growing up. She has always been accepting of my own family and me. She is a very wise, witty, and passionate lady. MS has stricken her muscles and limits her energies, confining her to her "quarters," as Dad used to say. However, she orchestrates life around herself in amazing ways and keeps it as normal as possible.

Her positive outlook, given her extreme limitations, is inspiring. She helped get my house clean when we were preparing for the Stem Cell Transplant by providing the means to hire some help. She is a creative, resourceful lady and another of the treasures I have in my life.

Six months later, March of 2012, our son had another major surgery to correct the blood flow in his brain. And within months of the brain surgery, he needed an emergency appendectomy.

In late summer, five months later, I was headed to the doctor for the first time with an unusual backache. The testing began, resulting in the eventual diagnosis of Multiple Myeloma. (And the beginning of this journey!)

For you, reader, the hike up and down the cliffs of my family history may have been tiring, but we have come, full circle, back to the flow of the journey.

All these situations have been preparing me for this current season. Life gives many lessons along the way. I can now say, it has been a privilege to learn about life in the *good hard* lessons of loved ones dying and major shifts in our family. But there were many days I wanted all this "hard medical stuff" to go away. As if I could wake up from this bad dream and have everything back to normal. Obviously it doesn't work like that.

The gates of heaven have been a "turning back point," so far, in my life. One day I will get to walk through those gates, as the Good Lord will call me home. In the meantime, I will continue to live life with hope, celebrate the treasures I find along the way, even if there are major shifts. Jesus will show me how to walk with others, as we all get closer to the gates of heaven. And the treasury of my heart continues to be filled.

Bee Still

Compared to the Grand Canyon, the back yard seems strangely still and quiet at first glance. The afternoon sun is peeking through the trees and the warm August air is pleasant and inviting. Sitting down in the reclining deck chair, away from the cold air-conditioned living room, I try to blend into the scenery.

Watching…

Waiting…

I know there is more going on here than I realize, so with time set aside to "be still and know"…

I keep watching!

As I finish my lunch, the wind rustles through the trees. Then there is a shuffling sound. Looking up, a leaf is waving back and forth, brushing up against the neighboring foliage, creating a new rhythm. Nice!

Memories flood in of younger days with kids resting under the trees and giggling about how the tree is saying "hi" in the "wave" of the leaf. Fun!

A pair of little white butterflies dance through the yard,

followed by little tiny bugs, maybe "No-See-'Ems" at least for now, "No-Name-'Ems." The sun shines off their tiny wings sparkling as they move through the yard.

The dragonflies are higher up, not coming down into my space today, but coasting on the air above. Must be a fun summer ride.

I don't recognize the jumbo-bumble flier that is sharing the high air with the dragonflies, but I am glad that it is staying way up there. It's one scary looking flying bug.

Occasionally, there are birds that call to each other from the tops of the trees, waiting for the answer and then responding once again.

A little masked Nuthatch flies into the birdbath. Landing on the water piping, he slides closer to the reservoir, pausing to look around to make sure the coast is clear, then sliding in for a quick drink. He stays for a moment. Then flies away.

The spider webs are like vertical trampolines, glistening in the summer breeze, with the hunter smack-dab in the middle of the web waiting for dinner to jump on.

A young robin first lands on the fence, then after a quick "Lab check " (the dogs are asleep beside me) hops down into the grass and begins hunting for worms in the cooler shadows of the damp lawn.

And I thought the yard was quiet and still – hmmmmm, silly me!

The breeze shifts and the light smell of Jasmine floating my way is soothing. What a sweet fragrance.

I know crows have their place, but they are not my favorite creatures. They remind me as they screech overhead. The dogs are awake now, and alert. As one of the crows lands on the fence hidden by the apple tree, the dogs tense. Then, as if on cue, both Labs dash off the deck and scare the big black bird away. Good dogs!

My eye catches the hanging flowerpots that had received

"hair-cuts" in late July, with hopes of new blooms lasting into September/October. It's always hard to cut off all those long, trailing, blooming strands. But knowing that the plant might have a longer growing season, I cut them. Now the blooms are budding out. Welcome back! Missed you!

From my deck-side vantage point, I can see our fence that runs along the two visible edges of our property. There are several maple trees fully leafed out and standing tall above the yard. The deck has been finished off with a high-extended set of timbers that allows the hanging pots to dangle nicely over the railing.

All remains still….

Until…

The local squirrel decides to use this network of fence edging, tree-limbs, and high timbers for his "superhighway." He scampers and jumps from one foothold to another with ease, never touching the ground, yet sending the dogs into "orbit." All chaos breaks out…dogs bark, squirrel chatters, leaves shifting, paws half way up the trunk… oh my!

Whew…

The dogs finally give up, plopping down again on the deck. They keep one eye on the hiding squirrel while trying to doze off into another nap. Quiet is restored.

The sun has slipped down and the temperatures are forcing me to go back inside. The slight breeze that is still sneaking through, every once in a while, catches the clapper on the wind chime and hits one of the pipes, sending a sweet ding through the night air.

It's amazing what I can see if I keep watching and can be still!

In fact, a few days later I watched a swarm of 8,000-10,000 honeybees fly into our yard and land in our Pom-Pom tree. We were told the queen must have been on the move and her loyal followers came along. Their forty-eight-hour visit was remarkable. They left as quietly as they had come.

📧 Sent: Saturday, July 13, 2013
📧 Subject: Next Chapter July 13, 2013   Plan C /New Treatment Starts

Hello Stomping Team,

I may not be out of the woods but there are sure some beautiful things to see and smell here. The ground is covered with thriving plants and flowers. The fragrance is amazing. And the birds and the bees have their own way of dancing through it all, praising the Lord. I am honored to join in the chorus.

We saw Dr. Onc yesterday and started, what we are calling, "Plan C*." (We'll do the whole alphabet if we need to.)

Bottom Line: Started new Chemo/treatment

Plan A –Treatment: Oct '12-May '13- hit partial remission for <1 month.

Plan B: Stem Cell Transplant - on hold - MM (Multiple Myeloma) counts too high

Plan C*: Treatment #2 - July -??? (Oct-Nov) whenever counts trend down again and we hit remission (< 100 in the MM/ light chain #)

Plan D: Revisit Stem Cell Transplant idea/maintenance of remission

Dr. Onc said this treatment (Plan C) is not too harsh and given my age and otherwise healthy state, I should tolerate this treatment just fine.

The first day is probably the most challenging....

> an injection
>
> 20 chemo pills
>
> assorted anti-symptom prevention meds

I can say, now after twenty-four hours of my first dose, that the fight or flight feeling has now settled and the three-hour morning nap helped the lack of sleep through the night. I've kept all my food down and enjoyed many glasses of water!!! (And the effects that go with all that water.) All in all, it's a mild reaction. Thank you, Jesus!

Dr. Onc is still pleased with the **kidney numbers**...somewhat surprised in the delay, but hopeful they will continue to get better. The **MM numbers** are still trending the wrong direction.

Along with the physical healing/treatments and believing God for His miraculous encouragement to continue, I am working on some emotional healing, filling some emotional holes from some childhood hurts. The goal: *to be whole.* I *say* that God loves me, but to really *know* that the Lord delights in me, that He really likes me, is another process!!! Sometimes I think I've got it, but then I start doubting and try to *do enough and be good* so He really *can* love me. The truth just leaks out. There's a hole in my emotional bucket. I'm working on it!

Prayer requests:

> Healing from MM - (Why can't I be the first?) and give

Him Glory!!!

MM counts to drop.

Kidney function to improve (<1.0). Doc doesn't think we'll get to that number, but **nothing is impossible for Jesus!**

Cement the hole in my bucket so I can be whole.
Health during treatment: poison of chemo affects only the bad guys.

Praises:

Bare feet on warm pavement, dog whiskers that tickle, empty bins from a successful garage sale, can opener ministries, Jasmine tunnel of fragrance, sunny days, watering systems, re-stained deck, comfy deck chairs, helping hands, healthy teeth-no root canal, pampered feet, flexible schedules, birthday greetings, play money, calls, notes, texts, meals, smoked salmon, wilderness journeys, amazing, caring, people... patience given. Thank you, Jesus!

In Good Hands,
Jeri

Sent: Wed, July 31, 2013
Subject: Next Chapter July 31, 2013 Into Rhythm/Moving Along

Just checking in....no real changes to report.

An observation:

Rhythm* is everywhere...

-The beat of a drum

-A clap of the hands

-The heart beat

-Sunrise - sunset

-Ocean waves surge -retreat

-Stop and go of traffic lights...**rhythm**: it helps us move along.

After three weeks of medical blasts we are learning the **rhythm** of this treatment. It's helping us move along.

> Jesus said, "Walk with Me and work with Me – watch how I do it. Learn the unforced rhythms of grace" (MATTHEW 11:29 MSG).

Bottom line: Round 1 of Plan C is moving along fine. Three of the four treatments - complete.

Rhythm - Medicine Blast:

> Friday morning: twenty pills with "Glug-Glug." (Oatmeal, as my Grandma use to call it.)
>
> Friday mid-day: injection usually followed by Chai Tea, my after-treatment treat!
>
> Friday night: tired, yet wired - sleep will come, learn to rest
>
> Saturday: productive morning...sleepy afternoon
>
> Sunday/Monday: naps are good
>
> Tuesday/Wednesday/Thursday: increasing stamina yet still at a much slower pace than I've ever known

Repeat for 28 days

See the Doc - start next round

I can tell you it has been an emotional few weeks. I can't say why. I just keep the Kleenex box close. I have found myself laughing with tears, crying with tears, just sitting there and the tears come...hugged in a quilted embrace with tears. There are aahhh-haaa moments that God is soooo near and loves me with tears, reading a book; you guessed it, with tears. Watching the moonrise, with tears.

Then the more obvious, in the dressing room with the next size up with tears, medical weight is not so fun. Surrendering to the fact that substitute teaching in a school environment with all the viruses/germs is just not a good idea; door closed, tears. I'm sure God has His plan for me in this quiet place. "Be Still And Know." ...tears. "Not my will but Yours"...tears. They say tears are cleansing, maybe they are cleaning up all the junk on the inside, MM and Creatinine get washed away, the hole in the bucket getting filled and cemented in with God's love.

I can borrow the phrase, but as the DJ on the radio said,

> "Do not borrow trouble from tomorrow by worrying about the future; live and enjoy today."

Soooo, I have been picking berries...berries on a hill, berries on a farm, berries along the road, and berries in my back yard. My freezer is filled with plump fresh berries. There have been river runs in the sun, BBQs, lake hikes with a butterfly chorus and ice cream stops, reassuring conversations, hugs, cards, notes, texts, prayers, stories, crab from my fisher-man, amazing seed pods replacing a cascade of purple flowers...a Rhythm of thanks...the bells are ringing!

Thanks for listening...I feel the support!

In Good Hands,

Jeri

Butterflies

As an egg hatches into a caterpillar, a very hungry little creature crawls over the leaves and branches of its new habitat, eating its way up one branch and onto the next, enjoying the freedom to move about the world as it chooses.

Along the way, the not so hungry, not so little caterpillar slows down, full from its munching, and clings to one leaf. Once attached, the caterpillar hangs, safe, suspended, dangling over the ground. Does a caterpillar know when the days of the cocoon are approaching?

It seems to be preparing.

Is it curious?

Is it afraid?

Is this a frantic, hurried process?

Is it just curious and hungry?

And when the caterpillar is all wrapped up in its cocoon, still, isolated and enclosed from the outside world, does it feel like chaos in there as the changes are taking place?

Transformations ARE taking place, yet are unseen to the observer. There is a waiting…and more waiting. As time goes on, there are a few wiggles and twitches that shake the cocoon and the branch on which it's hanging.

Is this a struggle, growing pains?

There seems to be pushing, stretching, tugging, and straining, a fight to be free of the "little wrapper."

Is it true that assistance would be crippling at this point?

Is this something the creature and the Creator are doing alone?

Finally there is an emerging of the butterfly. It is tired and hangs for quite a while, resting from its entry into the world. The wings dry out, spread and fill with life-giving blood. The butterfly tests its flaps. And rests some more.

Filled with new life, strengthened and seemingly encouraged to take flight, the butterfly flies away, free to move about, once again, into the world as it chooses. It soars into sky...

Changed forever by the unseen Hands of The Creator.

There are transforming seasons in my life.

Times when I wander about, on the ground like the caterpillar, going wherever I please. At some point there is a realization that I'm lost, there is a change coming, or I missed an opportunity. God stops me, much like the cocooned caterpillar.

The transformation begins.

It DOES feel like chaos at times; however, I'm very aware that He's up to something bigger than me. I'm learning to trust my Creator. Many times there isn't anything anyone else can do for me in this process. I get to press on, push, twitch, struggle, rest, "bee" and fight to be free. I rest and gain strength. And rest some more. And at just the right time, with a surge of Life within me, I take off and "soar."

Changed forever by the unseen Hands of The Creator.

**"Just when the caterpillar thought the world was over,
it became a butterfly."
(quote on a refrigerator magnet.)**

Side Note: Mom's collection of butterfly pins was made into a banner and hung in the hospital during the SCT to remind me that *new life* would someday emerge and I would soar again.

📧 Sent: Sunday, August 11, 2013

📧 Subject: Next Chapter August 11, 2013 Numbers Talk/Both Numbers Down

Hello again,

With our stomping shoes still securely tied on, we are doing another happy dance. Stomping on the *dis-ease* and celebrating that both the MM (Multiple Myeloma-Kappa Light Chains) and kidney (Creatinine) numbers are down!!! Thank you, Jesus!

Dr. Onc was very pleased when I saw him on Friday. "Medicine seems to be working very well," he said.

Bottom line: "Keep pushing the counts down as far as we can, then talk about Stem Cell Transplant (SCT). The SCT will bring a long lasting remission."

I have to be honest, when we talk about SCT, I'm still a bit hesitant. Okay, scared. I feel good right now. The process of SCT makes me feel "not so good, okay, really crummy, for a while." It's difficult to wrap my head around that exchange.

But as Dr. Onc reminded me,

> "This *dis-ease* gets more resistant and aggressive over the years and if we take it down to its lowest levels early on... more life!"

He also said that there are new things (medicines) that are "coming down the pipeline" that look promising. He hopes that during my lifetime that I will be able to take advantage of each treatment that is available to fight this *dis-ease*.

Because I do feel so good, I have to keep reminding myself that there is a battle going on. Just when I think, let's forget the whole thing (SCT), I am reminded that it really isn't about me; there is a process, a journey that I am on. As a result I get to connect with people in ways that I would never have connected with in any other way. I trust in my Great Physician and He has put me in touch with a great team of people. I get to share the story, so God gets the glory. Who knows, I may walk out of this cured of MM. Why can't I be the first one? But if not, I know if this is the "thorn in my side, His grace is enough."* There is life to live and things to do and people to love.

Prayer requests:

MM numbers continue to drop...normal 15

Creatinine numbers continue to drop...normal <1.0

Peace/confirmation from God about SCT

Continued health

Cure for MM

Thank you so much for listening and stomping along!

In Good Hands,

Jeri

> *To keep me from becoming conceited,... (I) was given a thorn in my flesh, a messenger of Satan, to torment me. Three times I pleaded with the Lord to take it away from me. But he said to me, "My grace is sufficient for you, for My power is made perfect in weakness"
> (2 CORINTHIANS 12:7-10 NIV- emphasis mine).

Colors Of Change

HOPE!

Promises Hanging!

Stem Cell Deep Freeze

City Lights From The
Medical Hotel

November Poinsettias!

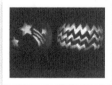

Sending You Hugs!

Do You Have A Moment ?

SECTION 6: FALL TO WINTER - 2013

Thanksgiving Reality

Progress...

✉ Sent: Saturday, September 07, 2013
✉ Subject: Next Chapter 9-7-13 Under 100/MM #'s Drop

Hello Stomping Team,

Thanks for all that you do!

Partnering with The Great Physician...we're "gettin' er done!"

Bottom Line: MM counts fell below 100!!! Dr. Onc wants to finish this newly started Round 3 of Plan C and start talking to Dr. OHSU (Stem Cell Transplant doctor at Oregon Health and Science University) in mid-October.

"Hooray...but gulp!"

As a side note, both Dr. Onc and Dr. Kidney are pleased with the overall lower Creatinine numbers/kidney function. Thank you, Jesus! And I'm sure lots of water helps, too!

Spending some time deep cleaning things at home, preparing for a "future isolation/clean recovery season." Enjoying the beginning of the autumn colors being painted all around and the yummy vine-ripened tomatoes. Oh, and my first attempt at growing brussel sprouts is about ready for harvest.

There are things all around reminding me that I'm not the one in control! The loud booming, lightening storms, falling leaves, season changes, shorter days, unpredictable alcohol ink, hair growth, MM counts...

Trusting the One who is in control and "learning to appreciate the end results"! I'm living life!

In Good hands!
Jeri

✉ Sent: Saturday, September 28, 2013
✉ Subject: Next Chapter 9-28-13 The Ball is Rolling/SCT Talk Talked

Hello again,

The yellow ball of the sun dips further away. The once bright morning walks are changed to catching the light from the full moon and twinkling stars.

Bottom Line: We have word that the Stem Cell Transplant (SCT) ball has begun to roll.

I don't have the medical itinerary for SCT, but the coordinators from my Oncology office and the OHSU office are working on my case again. By this time next week we should have a much better idea of the timeline.

I see Dr. Onc next Friday, October 4, and will get another set of Light Chain test results (MM).

Creatinine numbers dipped to an all time low and then went back up again. **My** un-medical theory is that there are soooo many Multiple Myeloma cells (Kappa Light Chains) being destroyed and sloughing off that my kidneys (Creatinine number) are working extra hard.

This thought keeps running through my mind. As I process the SCT possibilities, it is amazing to see how it all parallels the life, death, and resurrection of Jesus. In a mysterious kind of way, I am taking great comfort knowing that as the life I know literally comes to a "death," after some time there will be a "resurrected life" that slowly returns. (Jesus had resurrected life in three days. They say SCT is about a 100-day process, gaining 1% each day.) But because the blood counts go so low from the massive chemo I will hang onto a thread of life. My immune system will be wiped out and hopefully the Myeloma. I will be close to death, very weak and tired but in a "bubble of protection." After a two-to-three week stay in the hospital, I will be released to the safety of my home and my caring husband and family.

And just like my Lord...I will rise again!!!

There is hope!

FYI: Because of my immune system being so compromised in the beginning of this journey, there will be some huge precautions:

No visitors.

No crowds.

No live or silk plants...pictures of plants are good.

No outside food. Canned/frozen food only fixed at this house . (Fresh will have to wait. Glad I filled the freezer with summer goodness.)

This is the short list!!!

In the meantime I am enjoying a fresh coat of paint rolled onto bathroom walls, throwing the ball for each of the dogs, watching the "circle crops" go by on a short flight back home from Eastern Oregon, black and white soccer balls kicked by some amazing young ladies, new baby all bundled and rolled up tight, alcohol ink rolling around on the paper, bright orange pumpkins peeking out from the garden tour, the smile from seeing the round plate of hot apple and crust coming out of the oven, help for around the house deep cleaning, warning lights and buzzers to signal when the tire is NOT round anymore, special contacts rolling in, visits, calls, letters, emails, prayers, stomping. The little things when rolled all together make a big difference!!!! Thank you!

Praying for a "blood makeover," supernaturally reformatted life-giving blood.

The doctors have an intensive plan to help that happen, but my God can do that at any time, anywhere. I'd like more than anyone to roll on past this SCT and all its side effects. The ball is rolling. Not my will, but Yours God. I know You are here with me. Thank You for keeping me...

In Good Hands,

Jeri

✉ Sent: Wednesday, October 9, 2013

✉ Subject: Next Chapter 10-9-13 Color Bursts/Bone Morrow Biopsy

Hello Stomping Friends,

I really do enjoy all the brilliant colors that are literally EVERYWHERE right now. Shades of brilliant reds, fluorescent yellows, rusty oranges, deep magentas, spectrums of greens and browns and sometimes mixed all together. And every day is different. God has an amazing paintbrush, and is on the move.

The doctors are on the move, too, but at a slower pace than I earlier thought.

Bottom line: Bone Marrow Biopsy October 31

Dr. OHSU wants to get a bone marrow test and results back before setting any dates on the calendar. So at this point IF the numbers are where he wants them and IF we get a green light then mid-November for SCT (Stem Cell Transplant).

It's really all just "wet cement."

(I'm really okay with waiting and watching what God is doing all around me. It's pretty wonderful on lots of levels.)

God's on the move with the numbers too...

Creatinine numbers hit another all time low!!! 1.67

MM numbers are also a bit lower!!! 93.3

Thank you, Jesus!

Everyone that I talk to in the medical world says that my hair WILL fall out with the SCT. My common response is, maybe it will, BUT, I'm still bringing my shampoo and hairbrush to the hospital. (God gets to decide.) And yes, I do have some hats and scarves and will happily share if I don't need them.

I am thankful for ringing phone bells and unique opportunities to quickly explain and then ask, "What are YOU thankful for?" I am thankful for hugs from both of my kids at the same time, "pie coaching," special chats, shared driving, room transitions, five hat days, Diamond Girls, sparkling butterflies, frogs singing in the dark, scavenger hunts, surprise boxes, turning the heat on for the first time of the season, boxes of "history", sunny walks after a deluge of rain, hearing the pitter-patter of drops on the leaves, being safe inside...warm and dry...when it all comes pouring down, and then watching the rainbow, full of promise, tie up the sky.

Thank you for listening and stomping.

He's in control and has me in...

Good Hands,

Jeri

📨 Sent: Saturday, October 19, 2013

📨 Subject: Next Chapter 10-19-13 Wet Cement/SCT Itinerary - Maybe

Hello Stomping Team,

Wet cement is a messy kind of dilemma. Nothing is really set up and while waiting for it to solidify, it can be "reworked" or stepped in and that can change everything. However, before getting the job started, there is a form in which to pour the wet cement.

I had a conversation this week with my OHSU coordinator to get some paperwork signed so my husband can be off from work to be my caregiver for the SCT (Stem Cell Transplant); she gave me that structure.

Bottom line: We have an itinerary for SCT...in wet cement.

Wet Cement Calendar:

Oct 25 Finish with Plan C...last chemo dose of Plan C/Round 4

They want two weeks clear of chemo before beginning what we will call Plan D/SCT.

Oct 31 Bone Marrow Biopsy

These test result numbers will determine if the cement will set up in this outlined itinerary. Kind of like Green Light/Red Light (Oh, that was a fun childhood game!)

Nov 4 Dentist check and X-ray

Nov 7 OHSU visit...special labs, "get ready stuff"

Nov 9 Growth-factor injections   @ home   (Neupogen)

Nov 10 Growth-factor injections @ home   (Neupogen)

Nov 11 Growth-factor injections @ home   (Neupogen)

Nov 12 Growth-factor injections @ OHSU   (Neupogen)

    + lab + collection of stem cells

Nov 13 Collection of Stem cells (4 hours)

Nov 14 Collection of Stem cells (4 hours) (if needed)

Nov 15 Collection of Stem cells (4 hours) (if needed)

Nov 18 Admit to OHSU Start mega IV chemo (Malphalan)

Nov 20 Transplant Day Rescued IV Stem cells returned to me

"Day 0" two-to-three weeks in hospital...recovery.

I must say it was unsettling to actually have dates on the calendar. Cold, clammy anxiousness came in waves.

In the past, I've spent many hours and days with loved ones as **care-giver** or part of a team of caregivers, learning as we went as to what needed to be done. At times, even spending the night to be near and to make sure things were going the way they should. As a "rookie", major **care-receiver**, I am discovering that the fear comes not from the actual SCT process, but from knowing that I won't always have my eyes open to see what is going on. I know my wonderful husband will have my back at the hospital, but what about when he leaves???

Oh, this is where The Lord and I had a long heart-to-heart chat.

I say...

"I've put my life in Your hands, Lord...I trust You."

Really????

This is a test.

Do I really KNOW that my life is in His Hands?

Do I really KNOW Him and how much He loves me?

Do I really trust Him to take care of me and be in control?

Surrender...tears...peace.

Yes, my life is in Good Hands, I am learning on a whole new level, that **He loves me and I can trust Him...no matter what.**

Lord, help me when I stumble.

Bright sunny walks help solidify my wet cement emotions. Our Creator is so amazing. As I walk about I feel like He keeps showing me things that He has created. I know it's not just for me, but on days like this, it kinda seems like it. I am thankful. Even the full moon reminds me that He never slumbers and in the O'dark hours of the night, the moon-shadows and bright stars seem to be helping Him keep His eyes on me.

And finding just the right moment in the day when the sun is rising in the east and the moon is setting in the west...

I am truly in awe.

I am in Good Hands,

Jeri

I am also thankful for connections to other SCT survivors, tea with friends, yard "fairies," early morning moon shadow walks, confetti leaves, color drives, catch-up phone calls and chance meetings, rides, texts, chai tea, ice cream, electric blankets, ah-ha moments, breaking chains, working filtering systems, deep conversations and cleaned spaces. Livin' life!!!!

Moon Shadow Walk

Wet Cement dates had been penciled on the calendar for the Stem Cell Transplant, including the final dose of Plan C-Round 4 chemo. However, after the weekly blood work, the MM (Multiple Myeloma) results were headed back up... again!!! It's very unsettling how a set of numbers can change my perspective on this journey.

I was very disappointed.

What?

And this was **with** treatment...ugh!

That's not fair!

However the message back from Dr. Onc was,

"You're still good to go for the SCT."

I found myself in the pits as the realization really hit again, that "this *dis-ease* does NOT play fair." The dis-ease was becoming resistant to the treatment. The ahh-ha of why the doctors had been pushing forward for a Stem Cell Transplant all started making sense. If SCT were done now it would hit the MM early, hit it hard and hopefully hit it deep into remission. Because it lurks behind the scenes, gaining aggressiveness to come back, the

SCT needed to get started. What a tailspin!

Kleenex please.

Let's just say I REALLY DON'T LIKE taking medicine. Especially knowing that side effects of the poison/chemo that is used to fight MM eventually start taking its toll on the body. I had been coming off a short break without any medications and had really been enjoying my off time. I was beginning to understand why people finally say NO MORE CHEMO!

Jesus HELP!

The routine early morning walks with the dogs was broken up with comforting hugs and a reminder that it's okay to have these kinds of days. I stayed in bed a little longer, was thankful for the closely placed box of Kleenex, and the timely connecting points with caring family and friends.

"I know it's not fun. We just have to keep taking it one day at a time."

"Yup, I know it's true, I just want to wake up and have it all gone!"

"Perspective is a funny thing. But we all have to take time to be upset about our circumstances so we can move past it and continue enjoying what we do have. The upset times are necessary! It's good to get it out! Then you can breathe."

My daughter phones from school,

"I love you Mom. Take some time and then take a hot shower, maybe some hot tea or something and a blanket. Cuddly things always help."

It's amazing how you can hug with words.

"Sending you lots of hugs today and always."

Caught 'em.

Later she sent me a picture of the pumpkin she had carved with a shooting star, trying to make something that would be comforting for the little ones walking through her "scary decorated neighborhood. Ready for October to be over."

Another hug.

The next morning, on our moon shadow walk, I looked up to see a brilliant shooting star. We were going through the darkened path from our neighborhood to the school. The shooting star streaked from east to west for at least ten seconds with its long bright tail filling the section of sky that I could see. My husband saw it and said it was the longest one he'd ever seen. It was soooo cool. And it did bring comfort. Even in the darkness, His brightness shines, giving comforting hugs of light.

It was a great reminder to look up when the path is dark.

My daughter responded, *"That's awesome! I told you I was sending you hugs!"*

You sure did send a great one, and I like your Partnership.

✉ Sent: Sunday, Nov 3, 2013

✉ Subject: Next Chapter 11-3-13 Shooting Star/Bone Marrow Test Complete

Hello Stomping Team,

As the nights grow longer, the days darker and many things are beginning to "sleep" for the winter, I was reminded that even in the darkness His brightness still shines.

Bottom Line: Bone Marrow Test is over...waiting for results

Let's just say this has been an emotional week. With MM number trending up, not playing fair and being resistant, my emotions took a spin. My hip was still extremely sore from the bone marrow biopsy. I was anxious and very unsettled, wondering if the SCT will really go this time. Downs and ups!

Kleenex please!

However the message back from Dr. Onc was, "You're still good to go (for the SCT)." And the message back from Dr. OHSU, "We need the bone marrow numbers to know for sure."

Waiting is not fun. Then the little whisper coming...

Do you trust Me?

<Deep breath>

Yes, Lord, I trust You.
Help me when I stumble.

Bone marrow tests are soooo not fun. They can only numb the skin. Once the needle gets to the bone I feel the intense pressure and extreme pain as the core sample is extracted. Guess I should take the full dose of pain medicine next time. The good news, I have REALLY strong bones. However that means it's harder to get to the marrow for testing...ouch!

That's all *behind* me now, with an ice pack, waiting for results and the "Green Light/Red Light decision." Results should be in by Wednesday or Thursday this week.

The way I look at it, the bone marrow test is probably the most painful part of this SCT process. The rest is all IV/Blood work stuff and recovery. And of course, lots of praying and stomping.

I am thankful for life and living it, Seattle soccer games, cheering tunnels, roaring falls, "DQ blizzard tests," color messages, cleaning team, a cleared-out garage that fits a car, Salvation Army drops, hot/cold sheets, suggested home worship nights when getting out doesn't work, friends that help sharpen iron, rides, soup, text messages, calls, notes, prayers, comfort pumpkins, deep smiles, doll home, new PJs, clean air, picture tours, trees losing their leaves...they stand tall and proud with or without their covering. I guess we'll see if I'll be deciduous or evergreen. Taking my shampoo and hair brush either way!!! And being thankful for the reminders that I'm...

In Good Hands,

Jeri

Thanks for listening.

📧 Sent: Wednesday, 6 Nov 2013
📧 Subject: Next Chapter 11-5-13 Green Light- mini/Go SCT

SCT is "a go"...more later after tomorrow's day at OHSU. It's nice to have an answer and moving forward.

In Good Hands,

Jeri

✉ Sent: Friday, 8 Nov 2013
✉ Subject: Next Chapter 11-8-13 Full-on Green Light/Countdown Begins

Hello Again,

WOW!!!! So many pieces to this puzzle and they all seem to be coming together. The wet cement has begun to firm up.

Bottom Line: SCT (Stem Cell Transplant) is going...actually in countdown...kinda like NASA -12 days ...and counting ...and praying ...and stomping ...and laughing ...and living life!!!

Thursday - Nov. 7   Day -13 (yesterday)
Events:

∞ Caregiver class: good information for patient and caregivers.

∞ Vein check: mine are small. They will use a catheter to harvest my stem cells.

∞ Social worker chat: she felt I was emotionally strong and would do very well.

∞ Labs: record number of vials (14) making sure I'm "healthy" and have a baseline to watch.

∞ Dr. OHSU chat: narrowed the list of side effects given my age, stage, and overall healthiness. Signed consent forms.

Other "takeaways" of what is ahead:

∞ Learning to count again....

∞ Day -11 (Nov. 9) Start growth factor shots.

∞ Day -8 (Nov. 12) Begin collection of Stem Cells.

∞ Day -2 (Nov. 18) Admit to Hospital.

∞ Day 0 (Nov. 20) SCT - IV – My stem cells given back to me.

∞ Day +6, +7, +8, +9, +10 are probably the lowest- blood counts, feeling crummy.

∞ Day +7 usually see hair loss - (still taking my shampoo and hair brush...time for a shorter look...."sassy" hair cut today! He's counted the number of hairs on my head and knows how many might need to be replaced.)

∞ Day +10 blood counts start to improve...which means strength starts...

∞ Hospital is like "Fort Knox"...helping me to be safe, rest, and heal.

∞ NO PLANTS/FLOWERS - I'm thankful for my yard through the window.

∞ Immune system will be compromised - limited exposure to everything!!!

∞ Wash hands - a lot...use paper towels.

Lord, help. This is scary and lots of information.

This is a " good hard " thing.

You're not alone.

Just pondering...

Metamorphosis

Hibernation

Migration

Molting

Seasons

Life

Cycles...changes...transformations...all of creation created to mirror the life, death, AND resurrected life of Jesus:

Life of a butterfly   Freedom, isolation, rest, FLIGHT
Life of a bear, squirrel, rabbit....
                           Roaming, darkness, still, AWAKE
Life of a bird -   Flying, distant, relocates, RETURN
Life of an eagle -   Perched, separation, molt, SOAR
Life of a flower -   Bloom, wither, dormant, NEW LIFE

I'm hanging on to this theme. The Bible says we are to identify ourselves with the death of Jesus AND His resurrected life. The process of SCT is ONE of THE closest things to actual death on this side of Heaven AND planned resurrected life. I will move from my freedom, roaming, blooming life to one of isolation, darkness, and separation. I will relocate, wither, molt, be still, and rest for a season. **But** then I will awake, return, re-bloom, take flight, soar with NEW LIFE and an expanded appreciation for what my Lord has done for me, how much He loves me, and is always there.

Thank You, Jesus.

Prayer request:

Healthy blood

Strong bones

Quickly multiplying CD34 cells (medical term for stem cells)... they want to harvest six million cells!!!

Normal temperature

Protection from infections

Settled stomach
Clear mouth/throat
Calm digestive tract
Healthy functioning organs
Improved kidney function
Open doors to share *His-story*. (I'm taking the Dolls with me!)
Peace
Sweet sleep
Life

Stomp request: (No Zone)
Multiple Myeloma
Bone pain
Fever
Infections
Mouth sores
Organ failure
Kidney failure
Closed doors
Fear
Sleeplessness
Death

I am thankful. The bells seem to ring on my phone just at the right time. Sometimes the bells need to be explained, a reminder to be thankful. I am thankful for singing friends, washed/anointed feet, forest walks, little world, bedside chats, lemon curd, and spiced bread, Christmas poinsettias and lights in November, bobbles, haircut parties, frozen pie, fires in the fireplace, peaceful home, amazing support people.

In Good Hands,
Jeri

Fog's Rollin' In

I really do think trials are a lot like the weather patterns. I can see the clouds building on the horizon, just like I know there is *something coming*. And as the storm clouds darken and the winds blow, my emotions can get thrown all around. The rains and the tears fall.

Then there are storms that *sock-in*. Fog comes thick and blankets everything. There is no visibility. Things that were once clear are hard to make out and blurry at best. Bearings are lost, no landmarks can be found.

A year into treatment for MM (Multiple Myeloma), the doctors put SCT (Stem Cell Transplant) back on the radar. The SCT conversation was dropped earlier in June because my MM numbers had climbed too high. The doctors really wanted to use the "transplant tool" and pound the MM into a deep remission. A *fear storm* began forming on the horizon. Thick fog rolled in as dates and procedures were penciled into "wet cement". Everything was getting blurry. The reality of this procedure was heavy and the landmarks I remembered from mom's transplants were scary at best. The layers of doubt grew thick; water droplets began forming in my eyes and ran like little rivers down my cheeks.

Where is that *feathered hideout?*

It's my *secret place* where I can take a deep breath and crawl up into the arms of my Father. I am quick to dash into its shelter.

Am I going to make it through this?

My Mom charted this territory. Do I have to go down this same path? Really?

Soooo not fun!

The doctors say that the transplant procedures have improved since Mom's. That's true. Even in the first month of treatment, my path was charted differently.

<Deep breath>

> *Take My hand I will lead you. I will lead you.*
> *It's going to be okay.*
> *I AM in control.*
> *I love you.*

The fog lifted a bit.

My emotions settled a bit, too. Peace is coming.

"*Even in the worst of storms and thickest fog, there is always blue sky up there...somewhere.*"

Alone in my room, electric blanket chasing away the clammy, cold, nervous chills, I hunkered down into the feathered hideout a little longer. I was actually feeling brave about the SCT procedure itself so...

What am I afraid of?

Over the years, I have been a *caregiver,* advocate and *on-watch*; alert and ready to step in when needed, for others. I was in control (not), but thought I had a handle on some of the things needed to care for my loved ones.

What was making me so nervous?

I figured some of it out. I was nervous knowing that during the SCT I may NOT be aware of everything going on around me; unsure of protocol and if it would be followed.

Would they take good care of me?

Would they pay attention to my needs?

Could I trust them?

And that was the short list.

I talked with my husband.

> *"I've got your back."*
>
> *"I'll be there for you."*

I was not so concerned about the times he would be there, but the times he couldn't be there. The emotional fog blurred my vision again. Finally I heard it. The Still Small Voice, like a brave bird that begins to sing somewhere close-by, yet is invisible.

> **I won't leave you!**
>
> **Trust Me.**
>
> **I'm in control.**
>
> **I'll take care of you.**
>
> **You can count on Me.**

I'm so sorry, Lord. Of course You'll be there.

I do trust You.

I can't do this without You.

I need You.

A few Kleenex later, the fog was thinning. The sun was actually dancing through the trees outside my window and casting happy shadows on the warm bed.

I got up, put on my sweats and walking shoes, and went outside. Blue sky everywhere, color bursting on trees and bushes. And as the wind blew gently through the trees, leaves fell like confetti. I could hear the leaves hit the ground.

You're in Good Hands.

📧 Sent: Friday, 15 Nov 2013

📧 Subject: Next Chapter 11-15-13 Collection/Stem Cell Collection Complete

Hello again Stomping Team,

Wow, what a week...

Bottom line: Stem Cell Collection...complete!!!

It's always good to look for the treasures in the up and down crazy storms. Here are a few storms and the treasures that I found this week:

Day -8   Tuesday, November 12

It was an early morning trip into OHSU for labs to determine if I had enough stem cells for the harvesting to begin. Sitting in a hideaway window seat we waited for results. We watched a couple hours of a foggy day roll by and a "leaf blower" move piles of fallen leaves. Red + yellow = a big pile of orange from a birds-eye view. It was worth the wait.

Good news; "She's a keeper!" Yay! Before they could start collection, they needed to place some "plumbing" into my neck. With a local anesthetic, I was able to interact with the doctor and nurses during the procedure, we were laughing. The nurses even put on a fashion show with their ten-pound, colorful, lead dresses that are worn during the X-ray part of the event. I left with tubes and a white dressing in/on my neck.

After a three-hour stay in the apheresis unit (the room in the hospital where the stem cells are harvested), I left with an additional knitted scarf around my neck that some local church ladies made. It was really nice as I was still getting used to the cold air that hits my neck after the "sassy-short-hair" cut.

Report: Harvest #1 - 2.32 million stem cells of the 6 million needed. We're on our way!(Dr. OHSU wants to collect enough stem cells for two transplants...one for next week and one for the future IF we need it.)

Day -7   Wednesday, November 13

Another early morning trip to OHSU and three-hour stay in the apheresis unit harvesting more stem cells. We met the lab technician that processes my stem cells after they are collected. She invited us to visit the lab later in the day. We grabbed some lunch and a nap in the car, waiting for the call that would let us know if we had collected enough stem cells.

Well, the news wasn't exactly what we wanted to hear. I needed to get a booster "growth-factor" injection before we left and come back in the morning for more harvesting. Also the MM (Multiple Myeloma) counts were really trending up now...280 up from 101.

<Deep breath>

We went for a walk in the fresh air and semi-sunshine. We found a rhododendron bush that was blooming. God sent spring flowers in the autumn, not to be confused with lingering summer flowers...hope!

We made our way to the special stem cell processing lab in His perfect timing. Shortly after we got there, a "timer" went off for the initial "cool down" of MY stem cells. We were there when MY cells were moved from a small freezer to a huge, liquid-nitrogen, cylinder deep freezer. This deep freezer is where the stem cells are stored until they are slowly warmed in a water bath and then used for transplant. Fascinating!

OHSU is located in the West Hills over looking the river city of Portland. The tram ride from the "hill" to the waterfront was even more spectacular on the way back up with the moon shining and the city lights coming on, the chai tea was good too!!!

Report: Harvest #2 - 1.51 Wednesday + 2.32 Tuesday = 3.83 of the 6 million stem cells needed. Shy!

Day -6   Thursday November 14

A VERY early morning back to OHSU and a 4-hour stay in the apheresis unit. Pre-collection lab work was looking good for completing the six million-cell goal, but also showed a low magnesium count. Neck "plumbing" catheters are good for importing things, too. So with the collection process complete and the magnesium on the rise, I was "wheel-chaired" across campus still hooked up to some drip lines to the cancer clinic/infusion room to wait for the final stem cell counts and more magnesium. We were unprepared for the "packed-like-sardine" room that was our waiting/treatment room. The staff was amazing and my husband and I made it through together, even though we both wanted to run!

Dr. OHSU stopped by in the midst of all this and discussed, in a private room, the plan going forward. We made our goal for the stem cell collection. Thank You, Jesus! He also reviewed the aggressive MM upward trend which went from 101 to now

280, just in two weeks without treatment, which is a higher number than when he put the transplant tool on hold in July. Rats! However, he decided to keep with the scheduled plan and use the Stem Cell Transplant tool starting next week. After transplant he wants to return to injection treatments once a week to keep this MM down as long as possible.

This is soooo not fair and disappointing.

<Deep breath>

A unit of platelets and 15 minutes of applied pressure to the now "plumbing-free" neck and we were out the door. Free, tired, and hungry, three-day weekend here we come!!! (And a celebration of an amazing caregiver's birthday!)

Report: Harvest #3 - 4.58 Thursday + 1.51 Wednesday + 2.32 Tuesday = 8.41 million stem cells.   (Aka: CD34 cells) Made our goal and then some!!!

At this point in the journey my husband and I have set up a Caring Bridge site. It is a private website that will be updated while I am in the hospital. Family and friends can follow along, praying and stomping as the journey unfolds.

There is a place where you can leave a message; however, I will miss the ability to personally respond to each of them. Please know how much I appreciate all the love, care, support and prayers...always a tangible reminder that I'm....

In Good Hands,

Jeri

Ttfn

Diamond Girl Story

The Dolls traveled with me. And the story evolved. When an opportunity came up I would ask,

"Do you have a moment? I have a story to tell you."

With the door open...I began:

When I was first diagnosed with Multiple Myeloma, it was like I was dropped into a deep dark pit. "Jesus Help!" was my prayer. And this is what came out of that.

(Bring out Dolls from a black cloth bag.)

This is a set of Russian Dolls. We modified them.

*The **Outside Girl** represents the collection of Cool Houle family scars.*

Our son has a prosthetic eye and wore a patch before his surgery to keep the light out of that eye. He had what they call Moya-Moya Dis-ease, where the blood flow to the right hemisphere of his brain was constricted. So they did a bypass surgery, taking an artery from his forehead and connecting it to a lobe in his brain. He has a scar on his head from the surgery. He also had an emergency appendectomy.

This is also where I get my treatments. It's a ten-second injection in my belly.

We all have scratches on our arms. She doesn't have arms, but we put scratches on her side. My kidneys have been affected by this dis-ease.

Our daughter has a scar on the back of her leg.

My husband has a scar on the back of his head from a rock game he played with his brothers.

Spoiler Alert: (And she's wearing a head covering like I did when I lost all of my hair because it's cold when you're bald.)

She's falling apart.

The **Glass Girl** *is made up of broken pieces of glass. She can be sharp and edgy – kinda "snarky," emotional at times: happy, sad, mad, afraid, frustrated - all over the board.*

I believe if I give God all my broken pieces, He can make something beautiful out of them.

I'm a work in progress.

Inside is the **Diamond Girl.** *Because Jesus died on the cross, He has forgiven all sins, healed all dis-eases, rescues out of the pit and is preparing a place in heaven for her.*

I believe that this is the part of me that God sees when He looks at me. Jesus died to give me life. It is a life that will last forever.

Nothing can touch the Diamond Girl.

When I tried to put all these pieces together, the dolls didn't fit back together. However, my brother-in- law taught me how to use a dremmel tool and carve out the inside. My sister-in-law taught me how to use glasscutters. And my son and I worked on the Outside Girl, 'cause we needed a distraction.

I realized that this was a process and I couldn't have done this project without help from other people. Just like I can't make it through this medical stuff without help from other people.

I shared this story with a group of women. And my friend who set up the breakfast decorated the tables like a Tiffany's Jewelry Store. Turquoise table clothes, big white ribbons and big plastic diamond beads all over the tables.

One of the ladies came up to me after I finished and suggested that when I share the story to share a "diamond."

So I want to give this to you.

And I hand a "diamond" to whoever is listening to the story.

Thank you for listening to the story and being part of the process – there is a Diamond Girl (or Diamond Guy) inside of you and Jesus Loves You!

The dolls and the diamonds went to the hospital.

Going Through
The Fog!

Morning

View From
Medical Hotel

Evening

Decked-Out
Tree!

Countdown
Chain

Day +15
Home!

Mission Accomplished!

Hair Today! Gone
~~Tomorrow~~ Today!!!

Early Signs Of
New Life!

Ticker-Tape Parades!
Celebration
Time!

Home For Christmas

Going Through The Fog!

The Stem Cell Transplant and the first two months of recovery were very interesting. There are some parts that I remember vividly. Some pieces are in order, but many are just a jumbled pile of partial days and memories. I've been told it is probably a good thing that some days, especially hospital days, I don't remember. I was in a really heavy fog.

The pieces are sketchy...

Okay Jesus, lead the way

> **...As a sheep led to slaughter, and quiet as a lamb being sheared, He was silent, saying nothing** (ACTS 8:32 MSG).

I will not complain, either. At least, I will try.

🖅 Here we go!
🖅 Written Nov 18, 2013 by my husband

Hands up take on a whole new meaning on this medical roller coaster.

November 18 – Day -2 Another early morning ride into OHSU. Bags packed. (Clothes, shampoo/hairbrush, toothbrush, craft projects, Ipad, the Dolls, quilts and decorations) They said to make my hospital room comfortable. Permission to pack!

However, before I could check into my "medical hotel" room, the line placement team needed to attach my Groshon, fancy name for the plumbing/tubes that would deliver meds, chemo and blood products in and blood draws/tests out.

I had checked into the "line placement unit." The operating room nurse, after hearing the "Diamond Girl" story, changed the radio station. The doctors didn't notice...yet.

I was draped in a blue paper tent and told to turn away from the procedure. They used local numbing medicine, so I was very aware of the process!

At one point the doctors were discussing the procedure and how to secure the device, when one of them asked,

"Who turned on that station?"

Their hard rock music, that normally goes unnoticed by patients under general anesthetic, was missing!

I'm not sure which local Christian station she had found, but over the airwaves came *"You're an Overcomer,"* my encouragement from God. Thank you, Jesus for this word and the distraction.

I found out later that the nurse thought I would appreciate the change in stations...she was right! (See *Letter to Mandisa.*)

With the second set of plumbing in place in less than a week, I was ready to go to my fourteenth floor room. The new hospital wing was "state of the art", but more exciting to me was the view from Room 4. Let's just say the city of Portland is stunning, especially at night. But nothing compares to Mt. Hood at sunrise. And with a two-to-three week stay in this room, I would enjoy the spectacular view.

On that first day, after the half hour mega dose of chemo, ice chips and popsicles, I decorated my penthouse suite. Out of my bags came Mom's covering quilt, my pillow, purple blanket, family photos, a butterfly banner, miscellaneous craft supplies, Christmas lights for the windows, Lincoln – the stuffed puppy, Sr. Francis – the bald eagle, Pipin – the flying pipe-cleaner pig, and of course the *Diamond Girl Story*- aka "The Dolls"; a comfy room with a view. Thank You, Jesus!

▦ Chemo Begins
▦ Written Nov 18, 2013 by my husband

Jeri is sucking on ice chips and Popsicles to avoid mouth sores. The chemotherapy will run for 30 minutes.

They say that keeping the mouth cold before, during, and after the half-hour mega dose of IV chemo can help prevent mouth sores. So, a half-hour before the chemo, the nurses brought me ice chips and popsicles. Burr! The cold constricts the blood vessels and doesn't allow the chemo to damage the area. I'd say the cold treatment worked okay for my mouth, but my throat, esophagus and the 20+ feet of my GI tract were shredded. Much like a cheese grater, one nurse described. Ouch!

Oh Jesus, this is nothing compared to what You went through. Thank You that You never leave me and in my weakness – I was so tired, exhausted and "out of it," I didn't even realize You carried me. I am forever grateful.

▦ Nausea Go Away
▦ Written Nov 19, 2013 by my husband

Jeri has been given both doses of chemo. Battling nausea.

▦ Stem Cells
▦ Written Nov 20, 2013 by my husband

11:00 Jeri will be getting her stem cells back. She is having trouble keeping food down. The nausea meds are making her sleepy. As usual, Jeri has taken every opportunity to share the Doll Story. Sure is great to see the expression on their faces as she hands them a plastic diamond and says, "Jesus loves you and thanks for being part of my process/story."

I remember being very aware of the door to my room opening and closing. Anyone coming in always knocked a couple of times. (Except for my husband, he would just slip in.) Even if I was asleep, I at least peeked at who was coming in. I was on a mission! I had told God I would go through this if He got the glory, even though for a while I just wanted to go *home*.

I'll get the glory if you tell the story.

I had a story to tell.

I would ask a new visitor,

"Do you have a moment?"

"I have a story to tell you."

There were a few times when my visitor needed to finish something before they could listen, but more often than not, they were ready to give me time to share the *Diamond Girl Story*. I would grab the black bag that held the story and take my visitor through, what has become *His-story*. I would thank them for being part of the process that was helping me through, give them a little diamond bead and tell them, "Jesus loves you." When my counts were low, I would put on cotton gloves to protect my sensitive skin from the sharp, and edgy glass girl.

I told the story a lot while at the hospital. I finished the entire 160-piece package of *diamonds* I had purchased.

I knew the Lord sent many of His helpers to me on a daily basis.

📝 Stem Cells are in!
📝 Written Nov 20, 2013 by my husband

Jeri just finished getting her stem cells. She had no issues. A question came up: Will the chemo harm the stem cells? The answer was that the chemo already did its job and was metabolized by her body. It is now gone out of her system. Doctor just came in and said the stem cells are in and already going to work making new cells. He says it will take some time before there will be enough cells to count in blood analysis. Jeri is now sleeping peacefully.

My stem cells were transplanted back into my system using a 60-minute IV line and the bag of thawed/processed stem cells. It was anti-climactic. But, I remember the doctors and nurses congratulating me once my stem cells were all "in." That was **November 20, 2013, aka Day 0.** They all seemed pleased.

Grow little stem cells grow!!!

📝 Day +1 Charlie is gone!
📝 Written Nov 21, 2013 by my husband

Jeri 's IV cart, Charlie, was disconnected today. Shower, walks, puzzles, art projects, and of course lots of diamonds being given away. A smile on her face marks day +1.

📝 Lookin' good
📝 Written Nov 21, 2013 by my friend

Jeri already got six laps of walking, I mean STOMPING, in today, which is over a half mile! She is amazing!!

When we first checked into Room 4, my admitting nurse gave us her "schpeel" (said with accent):

"Sanitize your hands when you cross through this barrier going in or going out."

I can still see her outlining the doorframe with her hands.

"We will be pushy with drinking and eating, but when you can't, we'll help you out with IV's. We'll set goals every day.

Shower

Walks

Fluid intake

We'll be pushy with walking."

Someone had measured the hallway and if I walked eleven laps around the entire 14th floor that would be a mile. (I did make a mile a few times.) I kept track of the laps with pipe cleaners on the rolling IV pole...aka Charlie. If Charlie went with me, I just moved a pipe cleaner each time I passed my room. The best part of lap-walking was on the north end of the hall. The public windows were like a huge postcard of the city of Portland and Mt. St. Helens! Gorgeous!!!

Also on the north end of the hall was a family room (and more windows). We worked a puzzle there a few times and on Wednesday afternoons there were crafts. Beads, paints, cards, scarfs, snowflakes, and a couple of wonderful ladies who invited me to join! What a great distraction and motivation to get up and go visit. It's amazing what happens when the focus is changed.

📧 Day +2

📧 Written Nov 23, 2013 by my husband

Jeri had another great day... shower, walks, food, and plenty of liquids without the help of Charlie. A few have commented that she doesn't look like a patient.

📧 Day +3

📧 Written Nov 23, 2013 by my husband

Another good day! Walked the eleven laps again today. Mouth sores are minimal. No nausea. "Coasting" as the doctor put it. He says there will be some mountain climbing in the days ahead.

📧 Day +4

📧 Written Nov 24, 2013 by my husband

Another beautiful day outside and she is doing well on this journey. Your thoughts and prayers are much appreciated. Jeri has had many comments on her quilts. She loves the fall colors of the leaves that the trees have been dropping and leaf blowers are gathering in piles. She's getting laps in and sharing diamonds.

📧 Day +5

📧 Written Nov 25, 2013 by my husband

Jeri is now officially neutropenic. She doesn't have any white blood cells to fight infections. For the next five to nine days ALL will be very attentive on her condition. A fever is one indicator for infection. A nurse was telling us that sometimes the brain produces a fever realizing it doesn't have any white blood cells so it cooks the bad guys. Our bodies are wonderfully made. She looks good. She is still smiling and getting up and walking.

OHSU is a teaching hospital with residents, interns, and fellows. The service doc and his/her roaming team came in daily, on rounds. All of a sudden there would be a room full of smiling people. The team congratulated me when my counts were neutropenic; white counts so low they were undetectable. Mission accomplished: We have destroyed the MM infected blood. At this point my immune system was shut down. I had lots of anti-meds on board with VERY careful monitoring and lots of prayers. And no toothbrush.

Thank You, Jesus, for the bubble of protection.

📝 She is Amazing!
📝 Written Nov 25, 2013 by my friend

Each day when I go to see Jeri, I am totally amazed by her! She is doing so good. So proud of her! When I left today she already had nine laps in! In the midst of all she is going through, she still remains positive and looking out for others. I know you all are praying and we are so grateful. Another specific prayer request is for her throat. It is really sore from the chemo and makes eating and swallowing difficult. Thank you again stomping team! We are all in this process together!

📝 Day +6
📝 Written Nov 26, 2013 by my husband

There are a few less pills today. They are too tough to swallow. -IV meds instead. Pain meds for the throat are making her sleepy. She's still as positive as ever. Doctor says she's right on track. He said to expect three to four more days like this. She has shown no evidence of infection. Just waiting for those new cells to start multiplying!

📝 Day +7
📝 Written Nov 27, 2013 by my husband

No sign of white blood cells and the neutrophil count is zero.

These should start coming up in the next few days. They hooked up a pain pump to allow her to control it a bit more. She was flirting with a fever this morning but she is back to normal. She looks like she is feeling better today. Resting peacefully. Thank you for all the prayers and encouraging messages. They are helpful to Jeri and the rest of our family.

📧 Fever
📧 Written Nov 27, 2013 by my husband

Jeri has a fever. Blood draws from the lines and arm. X-Ray of lungs next. Looking for any signs of infection.

I don't remember much about these days. But I do remember there was such an amazing team of people that walked through my door, sanitized their hands, rolled up their sleeves, and helped me in this SCT (stem cell transplant) process.

Among these people were the nurses, dressed in scrubs, who, night and day, administered meds, fluids, answered questions, took vitals and kept a very close eye on EVERYTHING. When they noticed the pills were too hard to swallow, they switched me to an IV option. And *Magic Pink Mouthwash* was another option, which numbed my painful throat.

The nurses were even there when bodily fluids were out of control.

One night, in the O'dark hours, and I had physically made it to the bathroom, but I was a mess. With tears flowing, I found the pull cord...

"I need help!"

The nurse somehow knew when she came into the room that I needed a change of clothes, but she knelt beside me, rested her hand on my knee and spoke to my broken, humbled heart, then got the P.J.'s.

"It's gonna be okay, I'll help you get cleaned up. You're gonna get through this. It's gonna get better."

Thank you, Jesus, for sending your helpers in scrubs.

I also remember the doctor's team coming in everyday. They'd ask how I thought I was doing and if I had any questions. Even though I felt awful, weak, and out of control, they'd check me anyway. My throat hurt, I had diarrhea and a bucket next to my bed for the unpredictable vomiting. I was mostly unaware of things going on around me. When the team came in I was always sleepy, but this was part of the plan. They would check how I was doing with my goals. Then they listened to my lungs and heart in tandem, using two stethoscopes at once and parted with words like...

"You're doin' good."

"You're coasting along."

"Right on track."

"No points for being miserable, it's okay to take the meds."

"Benadryl is your friend."

"Hang in there."

"White counts are starting to come in...just ready to turn a corner."

Really?

If you say so!

The team's five-minute visit was very reassuring and the nurses reinforced their conversation the rest of the day. Thank You, Jesus, for wise, timely encouragement.

Jesus also sent in traveling diagnostic personnel who wheeled their equipment into the room, housekeeping, food service, massage volunteers, craft volunteers, even a notary that signed some official papers for us. And who knows how many others were out in the wings helping this process – pharmacists, lab techs, chefs, laundry personnel, and x-ray techs... amazing! Thank you, Jesus, for orchestrating this process.

✉ Normal temperature again
✉ Written Nov 27, 2013 by my husband

Jeri is resting comfortably. Nurse checked her temp and she is back to normal.

✉ Day +8
✉ Written Nov 28, 2013 by my husband

Happy Thanksgiving! We are grateful for your prayers and words of encouragement. Jeri is powering through this predicted rough spot. Blood tests from yesterday came back and one of the port lines had some bacteria. She has had a few blood tests today to be sure the bacteria were dealt a death blow by antibiotics. She has still managed to shower and take a few laps.

✉ Please keep praying
✉ Written Nov 29, 2013 by my friend

Hello stomping team!! Please keep praying for Jeri's throat/esophagus. -Very painful and difficult to swallow.

✉ Day +9
✉ Written Nov 29, 2013 by my husband

Jeri has been very sleepy. Nurse backed off a few of the drugs to help her become more alert. White blood cell counts are beginning to climb, a good sign that things are changing for the better. We're trying to find something that she can swallow.

Sometimes I wonder if mirrors should be allowed in hospital rooms. They can be startling. One day, after who knows what kinds of meds and chemo I had on board, I glanced into the mirror and I didn't see me. However, I did recognize the puffy face effects the meds/chemo had on me. It was like looking at my Mom when she was going through one of her Stem Cell Transplants. (She died in 2006 from a ten-year battle with Myeloma.) However, it was another good reminder and I could almost hear her say...

"'You can do this."

"One day at a time."

Oh, Mom, I really miss you!!!

Wow, my Mom and I really do have a lot common.

Another startling *mirror day* was when my sassy, short hair began falling out in handfuls. They all said it would happen. It was such a strange sensation to run my fingers through my hair and have a handful come tangled off in my hand. And it just kept coming. I was relieved, in some way. My hair falling out gave me something else to think about besides feeling really crummy. My husband said I was still beautiful. He said that a lot. I was too drugged to really care. But it was important to hear it. And, I'm still glad I brought my shampoo and hairbrush. I used them everyday. After this, I would just use the shampoo on my bald head.

(Just a side note: I did keep my eye brows and eye lashes throughout the entire journey. Thank You, Jesus.)

Yep, just like the fall leaves on a windy day, hair was everywhere.

Thank You, Jesus, You've numbered each one and know how many will grow back...in time.

My husband helped the process along and borrowed some trimmers. I'm thankful for hats to keep my bald head warm!

My son and my friend witnessed the trimming day; there's even a video. I can't say I remember anything but the cold on my head and being happy that hair wasn't coming out in my hands anymore. Showers became much easier and in time my collection of hats/scarves became a new way to accessorize.

📝 Day +10
📝 Written Nov 30, 2013 by my husband

White blood cells are at about the same level; they are busy doing their work. Jeri is still very sleepy. Doc said that in a day or two the pain will subside and she will get out of this drug-induced condition. Bad hair day, her hair has begun to fall out. She reaches up and runs her fingers through her hair and ends up with a handful. Doc said she is still right on track.

📝 Day +11
📝 Written Dec 1, 2013 by my husband

Jeri's white cell count tripled and neutrophil counts are now large enough to differentiate. The nausea drugs combined with pain meds are still knocking her out. When our son and I got here this morning, she was alert. Other side effects are lessening. I think this will be the last day she has hair. She has some cute hats to wear. I have always said that I like any hairstyle she chooses. She is still just as beautiful!

📝 Thank you!
📝 Written Dec 1, 2013 by my friend

Thank you all for praying! We couldn't do this without you! It has been a challenging couple of days, but today Jeri was doing better. We are beginning the climb out of the valley.

I knew the Lord sent many of His helpers to me on a daily basis.

My mighty warrior husband, and iron curtain was there everyday…a kiss, a hug, hall walker, bucket grabber, note-taker, reader, "Caring Bridge" writer, uplifting music player while I rested - hero. (I found out later he watched silent football games and listened to the music.)

My super son came to see me on his days off, spent Thanksgiving in the hospital, worked on a "flying-Cincy-pig project" that my daughter had sent. We even planned out and started writing "Pipin The Flying Pipe-Cleaner Pig" story. He walked the halls with me, squeezed my hand, and stood strong.

My delightful daughter sent notes, texts, projects, and phone calls from her Ohio space. Her Christmas lights shone at night in my room. I missed her, but she was as close as she could be in the flying danger/flu season.

My devoted friend navigated to OHSU for a daily visit, walks, talks, and numbered day photos. We even put together a 100-link paper chain that my daughter had sent to help count down the first 100 days post transplant.

These three witnessed more of this crazy storm than I did.

My joyful sister-in-law brought in her cheer and binoculars. Dragon Boat teams glided through the river below. We got to spy on them. She was there, relieved my husband, and even ate dinner with me in my room.

🖅 Day +12

🖅 Written Dec 2, 2013 by my husband

Jeri may be heading home as early as Wednesday. Blood counts continue to rise. We will need to learn to manage her continuing issues/symptoms. She is still being treated with antibiotics and likely will need me to administer them at home. I can do it. She is getting stronger each day. Pain meds have been turned off since yesterday. She even tried a bit of real food this morning. She says her throat is not an issue now. She is sleeping peacefully at this moment. Thank you for your continued prayer support.

▣ Day +13
▣ Written Dec 3, 2013 by my husband

Jeri's counts continue to rise. She is still battling some symptoms/issues but the docs are confident that we can handle them at home. Me too! She says food does not taste the same but is trying to eat a little bit throughout the day. She gets stronger each day. Jeri is still sharing diamonds with new people she meets. Your prayers and well wishes here on Caring Bridge are so much appreciated.

▣ Day +14
▣ Written Dec 4, 2013 by my husband

The doc AND Jeri thought it best to wait one more day. Some of the symptom/issues are getting a bit better. Jeri is starting to handle fluids on her own now. Platelets have bounced up and down as well as the red blood cells. The white blood cells and neutrophils continue to climb. The house is ready. The dogs went to our regular kennel and got baths yesterday. It will be good to have Jeri at home. Thank you for your prayers.

▣ Day +15 Going Home!
▣ Written Dec 5, 2013 by my husband

Jeri is packed and ready. Her counts are good. She is drinking enough fluids that IV fluids may not be necessary. She still will need a couple days of IV antibiotics. They are enabling us to do this at home. Now we sit and wait to be discharged.

And again, the doctor team congratulated me when my counts were **high enough for me to go home – December 5, 2013, aka Day +15**.

My belongings got packed up and the nurses packed supplies…lots of supplies. My GI tract was still acting up and my immune system was immature. So, with masks, hat and gloves, wipes and pads and a pouch full of medications, we loaded up a cart and put me in a wheel chair. And off we went down the hall to the elevator. It was quite the sight. But I didn't care what anybody thought. I was going home!

Home Sweet Home!!!

We were able to drive the car right into the garage. I'm so thankful we got that cleaned up last fall. No raindrops on my head. Our yellow labs met me at the door with their happy greetings. I made a quick pit stop and climbed into bed. My own comfy bed felt soooo good.

Over the next few weeks, I went out only for masked return visits to OHSU for check ups. Otherwise, I was in our cleaned up home. I spent a lot of time sleeping or sitting up in a chair at first. I also used a treadmill to try and regain some strength. Lying around in the hospital bed and all the other stuff had zapped my muscles. I was told it would take one week's time for every day I was lying around in the hospital for my strength to return. Oh my, I had a long way to go…patience.

📝 Day +16
📝 Written Dec 6, 2013 by my husband

Went back to OHSU today. It is a scheduled appt. We will be going in twice a week for another three weeks. Most blood counts have dropped but that was expected. She is not getting the drug that boosts the body's production. However, her platelet count went up on its own, which is great. Doc said that she is right on track. Taste, nausea, other GI symptoms should settle down in the next week. The neutrophils are busy repairing twenty plus feet of innards that were damaged. She is happy to be home and trying to eat and drink. Jeri says thank you for all your support through prayer, notes, and messages here on Caring Bridge.

📧 Day +17
📧 Written Dec 8, 2013 by my husband

This was a quiet day. Jeri rested most of the day. She enjoyed the DVR recording, *"The Sound of Music"* with Carrie Underwood. This was the last day of the IV antibiotic. She wasn't getting enough fluids down on her own so I set her up with the IV fluids. She continues getting stronger.

📧 Day +18
📧 Written Dec 8, 2013 by my husband

Jeri's best day yet! She had a good night sleep. Got up and ate breakfast and then walked on the treadmill. She took a shower and then took a nap. Our son came over and watched a cheesy movie with her while I made it outside to pick up the "poopsicles" and rake a few leaves. Our sister in-law came to help out. Jeri was able to eat small meals and drink the two liters needed to avoid IV fluids. She decided tonight to begin to back off the nausea meds. Please pray for this decision to be successful.

📧 Day +19
📧 Written Dec 9, 2013 by my husband

A quiet day. Jeri woke up early and hungry. She ate and went back to sleep. Our son and I visited our friend's farm for a Christmas tree. We thought Jeri would appreciate having a tree. We will put the tree on the deck and decorate it, since she can't have one in the house. Jeri is enjoying the Hallmark channel's Christmas shows in between naps. Fluids were necessary today. She didn't quite make her quota. We have an appointment tomorrow at OHSU to check levels. Looks like the choice to back off some of the meds is working fine. Thanks for the prayers.

✉ Day +20
✉ Written Dec 10, 2013 by my husband

Jeri jumped up and walked on the treadmill this morning. Appointment at OHSU went well. Doc said she now has an immune system, although not robust. She can now brush her teeth since her platelet count has risen. Counts look good and she is right on track. We are very grateful for the stomping team.

✉ Day +21
✉ Written Dec 11, 2013 by my husband

Jeri is doing well. She is getting stronger each day. Meds are tapering down, as are any symptoms/issues. Days are becoming a bit more normal. She is eating, drinking, and sleeping good. She continues to enjoy walking on the treadmill, napping, and checking out the Christmas specials on television. Thank you all for your prayers. They are evident in Jeri's recovery.

✉ Day +22
✉ Written Dec 12, 2013 by my husband

Jeri needs to cut herself some slack. She really wants to get back at it. She walked on the treadmill this morning and her body revolted. She took it easy the rest of the day. There is an appointment at OHSU tomorrow. Pretty quiet day.

✉ Day +23
✉ Written Dec 13, 2013 by my husband

It was a bit of a restless night. Jeri is getting sore from the inactivity. She got up this morning and walked on the treadmill but with a little less gusto. We are presently sitting in the infusion room at OHSU. Her numbers look great. She is pretty close to normal range. Needed some magnesium but the doc said that should correct itself now that the other symptoms have gone away. She is down to a couple pills a day. She looks great! I'm not sugar coating this one. It's true I am extremely biased, but others have said she looks great too.

✉ Day +24
✉ Written Dec 14, 2013 by my husband

Quiet day. Jeri continues to get stronger each day. I am going to switch to updating on Tuesday and Friday. We will visit the doc at OHSU on those days. The days are not as eventful unless I mention the sappy movie watched each day.

✉ Day +27
✉ Written Dec 17, 2013 by my husband

Doc said that Jeri's counts look great. Friday marks day 30, the usual release date. I was pumped because we were out of there within 45 minutes and nothing was needed. Jeri, on the other hand, has switched to thinking about the light chain numbers. We won't be checking those until the first of the year. Please pray for peace and that the light chain numbers are normal rather than high. She continues to get stronger.

▦ Day +30
▦ Written Dec 20, 2013 by my husband

Jeri was waking up to a spinning room the last few days. Nausea returned but we were able to get it under control with meds. She turned the bells back on her phone to remind her to be thankful. She has walked on the treadmill most days. She has been looking around her front yard and is dreaming about when she can get back to playing in the dirt. Doc says she has to wait another 60 days to play in dirt/garden. She doesn't have to wear a mask but should avoid sick people. Labs look good again. Tuesday she will get the port removed as long as her numbers remain good. Her Creatinine has been 1.8 for the last week. This is higher than it has been since transplant but still well below the pre-transplant level. She continues to get stronger and it is visible. She looks happy and I sure am enjoying this concentrated time with her.

At Day +30 I was released to go out to restaurants, no mask needed. However, that idea was a bit frightening. I had just spent weeks in isolation, washing my hands constantly and wearing masks whenever I went out to the doctors to avoid contact with germs and infections. I was reluctant to go IN to an eating establishment. So my husband and I sat in the dimly lit parking lot with a hot box of pizza. We ate till we were full and then took a drive. There were Christmas lights up in the neighborhoods. It was a lovely date!

The other exciting thing that happened at Day +30 was the return of the toothbrush. No more little green sponges. I was also clear headed enough to re-read emails and Caring Bridge entries that were once foggy. Wow, amazing support! Thank You, Jesus!

📠 Day +34
📠 Written Dec 24, 2013 by my husband

We visited OHSU today. Jeri's numbers continue to look great. The Creatinine stayed at 1.8. The line was removed so a shower without a protective bandage will be an option tomorrow. She needed to stay upright for four hours so we took our time on the drive back home. We made several stops at stores that were open this afternoon. Next week will likely be our last visit to OHSU. Merry Christmas!

📠 Day +41
📠 Written Dec 31, 2013 by my husband

We visited OHSU today. Doc said all levels still looked good. Creatinine went up a tiny bit to 1.9. We have been getting out most days. We take walks in the neighborhood or in a store. Jeri is getting stronger and stronger. Happy New Year to you all!

📠 Day +50 Transitions
📠 Written Jan 9, 2014 by ME

Thank you so much for all the love, support and praying/stomping...priceless!

This week we transitioned from OSHU back to Kaiser. The good news is that the light chains have been knocked back to normal levels (17). Thank you, Jesus!!! Both Dr. OHSU and Dr. Onc (Kaiser) were very pleased. However, this isn't the cure. They are talking about doing maintenance treatment every other week. MM (Multiple Myeloma) doesn't play fair. We'll keep believing that the counts stay low for the rest of my life. We were startled with the discovery of a growth in my breast that grew in less than a week. It has been scanned, called a cyst, and will be watched. Dr. Ob/GYN was pretty sure it wasn't cancer due to the rapid appearance. I am feeling good and getting stronger every day. I have been walking with Ken and the dogs in the morning. I still hit the treadmill later in the morning. And then take a nap. Lots of lessons in pacing and patience...one day at a time.

In Good Hands!

In the first full week of January 2014, we transitioned from OHSU back to Kaiser. With the midweek appointment set, we were excited to hear how far the MM counts had dropped. We knew we had hit remission but that good news was a bit overshadowed.

In the O'dark hours after my husband's first day back to teaching, I lay awake in the warm covers. There had been a wayward string left from the "plumbing" in my right shoulder/chest. As I tugged, it came out. Yay, one less doctor visit. However with that same tug my hand had bumped into my right breast.

A lump.

A large lump…

NO!!! Really? Go away in Jesus Name.

Fear raised its ugly head and I quickly found myself imagining walking down possible future roads.

Is it cancer?

Surgery?

Will I lose my breast?

I didn't notice this before.

Where did this come from?

It must have grown fast.

I know my breasts are lumpy, but this seems serious...it's BIG.

Is this how I'm gonna die?

<Tears>

Should I wake my husband?

I moved closer and put my hand on his shoulder. He was sleeping peacefully. Telling him now would just send alarm and interrupt his needed teacher sleep!
I wrestled in the dark....

Are you done?

Will you trust Me?

I got this!

Oh Lord, I'm so sorry! I put my life back in Your Good Hands.

Yes, I trust you!!!

<Sweet sleep>

As the morning alarm went off, I asked my husband to promise me he would continue to pray for peace...

"Sure! What's going on?"

I poured out my new discovery and encroaching fears. He

remained calm. He agreed it hadn't been there a week ago. He had peace, which settled my emotions even more!
I will trust you, Lord!

I made some phone calls.
Dr. OB/GYN worked me in. She was very reassuring, took her time, and wasn't concerned.
"Sometimes life gives us speed bumps. We get to slow down and take care of people! Probably a cyst, but we'll get a diagnostic mammogram/ultrasound a.s.a.p."

Whew!
That was Tuesday.

Wednesday morning Dr. OHSU announced that the MM numbers were at 17: Remission!!!

Thank you, Jesus!

After hearing about the line being tugged out and the newly discovered lump, He did a quick check and confirmed these two things were NOT related! It was puzzling and he was willing to wait to begin maintenance treatment until AFTER we found out what this lump was all about.
Dr. OHSU had a picture of a sailboat on the wall. I took a picture of it. It was a good reminder to live life! When I looked at the picture, the sailboat looked like it had a spotlight over it. In the actual picture, the boat was not illuminated. But God knows the course He's taking me on. He cares about the desires of my heart! I'd come through the white water rapids first in the Grand Canyon and then through the Stem Cell Transplant. One day I will sail on a sailboat.

Wednesday afternoon that same day, Dr. Onc at Kaiser was also pleased with the MM numbers and said,

"I wanted to tell you the good news, but Dr. OHSU beat me to it!"

We laughed and celebrated the SCT success! He also said I was doing well and hoped for at least two years @ 17/MM#'s. We'll keep watching the numbers.

MM (Multiple Myeloma) doesn't play fair. They say it is lurking about and will come back more aggressive. BUT GOD has touched me! He loves me and I trust Him. He is able to wipe MM completely out of me. I leave my life in His Good Hands and thank Him for this day! He is doing good things.

Thursday morning the diagnostic mammogram/ultrasound confirmed Dr. OB/GYN's hunch…a cyst. It's large, but nothing to worry about.

(FYI – a few weeks later Dr. OB/GYN reevaluated the cyst and drained it. And drained it again a month later.) We'll *keep watching* it.

Thursday morning after the first appointment, there was an extra lab visit for a possible bladder infection…all clear. However, it did take me back into the clinic to confront an uncomfortable situation with the new lab tech. I decided to speak to her, one on one, about a recent visit that had me debating about going elsewhere. I told her how much I liked coming to this particular clinic; it was close to home, small and personal. After describing the unpleasant scenario, she apologized. I'll be back.

Friday – lots of extra sleeping!

What a week!

I'm in Good Hands.

January and February seemed to pick up speed. There were less naps and more energy for short spurts of things. Noticing spring starting to sprout; lots of red-breasted robins, perching and singing in our trees, daffodils blooming, puddle-bath-splashing by little birds, hair growth, (He knows how many need to come back), writing, cooking, making future plans – including nine days with our daughter and her roommate.

By Valentines Week, Day +86, I had *walked off* all of the do-not-drive medicines and took our son to one of his doctor appointments. My husband surprised me with an *Edible Arrangement* of chocolate covered strawberries. My doctor surprised me with the MM test results they had dropped to ten!!! And God surprised me with a ticker-tape parade to celebrate the end of the Stem Cell Transplant war.

The fog has cleared…

Ticker-Tape Parades

A number of years ago, I had an appointment with Dr. GI about some pain in my midsection. He must have seen beyond my physical pain, because he asked me to describe different seasons, ages, and stages of my life. In my perspective, at the time, I had internalized the childhood tough stuff on top of the current tough stuff and had myself a good case of emotional-stress that was presenting itself in my GI tract.

There was something in Dr. GI's validation of my drama that released this prisoner from captivity. I remember him saying that I had been through a lot. He called me a hero for making it through the battle and added, "We give ticker-tape parades for the soldiers that return home from the war. You deserve a parade, too." He sent me out the door with his card and on the back he wrote...

"Jeri is a hero."

In those days, I was running, rain or shine. Running partly for the exercise and partly for an escape, time to think and clear my head. On one rainy, windy spring morning I was processing life and remembering Dr. GI's comments.

God, please help me!

Moments later a strong gust of wind hit a row of trees full of spring blossoms right in front of me. The petals took flight and were twirling all around me...tears spilled from my eyes adding more moisture to my rain soaked cheeks...my first ticker-tape parade. I ran under and through the "confetti" with delight.

God had given me a parade! He was proud of me. (When I reached the end of the row of trees, I turned around and ran through them again!!!)

I have come to realize that God gives me parades all year long.

In the spring, He uses petals.

In the summer, He uses "helicopters."

In the fall, He uses leaves.

In the winter, He uses snow.

My Daddy God loves me. He helps me through the *tough stuff*. I am a hero!

He is my Hero!!!

In February 2014 - Day +95/post SCT, my husband and I were given tickets to a concert. (See "Overcomer" Story) To our surprise at the end of this concert there was a man-made ticker tape finale. We ended up covered with the little papers. What fun.

The next day, I found confetti in my purse and the hood of my jacket. I was reminded of Dr. GI's story about the soldiers coming home from the battle to a celebration parade. That's when it dawned on me...I had been through a SCT battle...the war is over!!! The SCT is behind me!!! I'm getting stronger everyday.

I'm in remission!!!

God reminded us in a BIG way:

It's time to CELEBRATE!

Reader, here the emails need to catch up to what you have already discovered. The real-time conversations bring a new dimension to the recovery season even though some things will seem repetitive.

📧 Sent: Friday, January 24, 2014
📧 Subject: Next Chapter 1-24-14 Sun Is Out/Normal Levels - Remission

Hello Again Stomping Team,

Thank you so much for all the love, support, praying/stomping...priceless!

The fog is lifting, and the sun is out. Signs of spring are popping up everywhere. And with careful inspection even the trees are showing signs of new leaf buds.

God's way of giving HOPE!!! Hope that the winter and hibernation will transition...death to life!

Bottom Line: The Stem Cell Transplant (SCT) was "successful"***. The Multiple Myeloma (MM) numbers have been knocked back to normal levels. (17)

Thank You, Jesus!!!

Next Steps:

Monitor counts and numbers, via blood work and bone marrow biopsies

Begin Maintenance Treatment next week, via small injection (Velcade) into my stomach. (This was one of the chemo drugs used in the past.)

Continue recovery from SCT...

Anti medicines

GI tract recovery

Muscle strengthening

Peach fuzz hair growth

Stamina increase

It's amazing what can be found when coming out of the *fog*. Everything seems brighter and clearer. And just like the trees, given close inspection, *hair buds* can be seen on my head!!! In the absence of the *warm covering*, I am enjoying a collection of hats and scarves and trusting Jesus with the number of hairs that need to be replaced. There is HOPE!

"Walking is the best thing!"

We went walking in the grocery store. We go slow and work together, but we're out and about. And when Day +60 came this weekend, standing in the produce section seemed like being in a candy store. Yippee!!! Fresh fruits and veggies are back on the menu. It may take some time for my body to be so excited about this fact.

The lessons for this season: Patience. Go slow. Pacing. Especially with reintroducing "fresh" to my diet!

But there is HOPE!

Like with any recovery, there are "good-up days" and "not so good-down days." This usually has something to do with my physical, mental, or emotional state. And yes, I do have Kleenex. However, no matter what kind of day it is, it is good to remember that my spirit, like a diamond, can continue to shine because there is HOPE and I'm....

In Good Hands,

Jeri

Thanks for listening.

***Successful: Doctors are hoping for a 2-4 year remission with the MM numbers remaining in the normal range (3-19). MM doesn't play fair. It has been known to linger and to come back, even more aggressively. However, I have a BIG God. He has touched me. He loves me. He gives me strength to do what He's called me to do. There is HOPE!

✉ Sent: Sat, 8 Feb 2014
✉ Subject: Next Chapter 2-8-14 Celebration/Dropped Lower

Hi Stomping Team,

We're doin' the "happy dance" with snow boots and gloves this week!

Bottom Line: (MM) Counts DROPPED to 10 down from 17. And kidney function is holding steady under 2.0. Thank You, Jesus!

With the roads snarled with snow, the scheduled appointment turned into a phone appointment. But Dr. Onc was still extremely pleased with the Myeloma counts dropping even further. The only instructions were to sit by the fire and read a good book...really?!

He doesn't know me very well.

How can you "sit" at a time like this? This news deserved a more lively celebration, plus there was SNOW coming down like crazy. So, after pulling the cross-country skis and boots from the attic and bundling up, I did the "happy ski dance" out to the fields behind our house.

There was an amazing hush and a transformed beauty to everything. I stopped to enjoy it. And I needed to rest. Okay, maybe a good book would be a good thing, but not until I get to the "hill." I should probably call it a short slope...a three second glide, but I made it! All those treadmill steps are paying off and that was way more fun and beautiful. Wow, I slept well that night. And with the snow sticking around for a few days, there have been more skiing adventures.

Thank you for all the prayers, stomping, and praising the Lord. Please continue.

I am thankful for: His touch, times for celebrating, birds singing in the storm, snowy fields, playful dogs with happy snow-filled faces, truck chains, skiing company, dinner with friends, hot soup, warm house, running water, for being able to take advantage of feeling good and getting stronger. I am...

In Good Hands,
Jeri

Surprise Tickets

Overcomers

Livin' Life!

Remission!

Mending!

Keep
Telling
His-
Story!

Landmark Day!

Strong!

100th *Link-On!*

SECTION 8: SPRING 2014

New Life At Easter

Connections

Saying *thank you* is something I was taught at a very early age. However, it's not always easy. Especially when the person to whom the message needs to get to is hidden behind agents, producers, and security personnel.

I was obedient to **write** the letter to singer, songwriter Mandisa, thanking her for her inspiration. (Her song, *Overcomer*, played over the airwaves while I was in the Operating Room just prior to the Stem Cell Transplant and during my hospitalization.)

Now the question was how to **get the letter to her**.

As a recording artist, she was on tour with Toby Mac and some others. She was coming to Portland in mid-February 2014. Oh…she'll be close.

I have a friend with connections with Toby Mac. Maybe my friend could get my letter to Toby and he could deliver it to Mandisa. Hmmmmm.

That way the **letter** wouldn't be lost in the sacks of mail that she receives.

Good plan!!!

However, after searching for my friend's contact information, all I had was an address. I had lost touch with her. However, a week before the concert, my son and I went for a drive with the letter, ready for delivery.

Driveway full of cars.

Garage door open.

Lights on.

Knock, knock, knock…no answer.

Knock, knock, knock…no answer.

Knock, knock, knock…no answer.

"Let's go mom, we can come back another time."
"One more time."

Knock, knock, knock…no answer.

"Rats…okay…"

Not really wanting to leave yet, I stalled.

Searching.

Praying.

Hoping.

There's got to be a way to get this letter delivered.

About that time a big, black rig drove up along the street in front of my friend's house. Turns out it was her nephew. After introducing ourselves, he went through the open garage and into the house. Only to quickly reappear, announcing,

"No one was at home. But, they are probably a couple doors down visiting one of their daughters."

Gotta love close families.

"I'll be right back."

Sure enough, my friend was there.

I explained what I wanted to do and asked if she could help me.

"Yes. I'm looking forward to meeting her myself."

I told both my friend and her nephew the *Diamond Girl Story* and handed them each a *diamond*. After exchanging phone numbers, my son and I were on our way.

A couple of days later, I received a text message from my friend.

"Hi Jeri, I have two tickets for you if you would like to go see Mandisa?"

"Oh my goodness…"

After talking it over with my husband and evaluating how strong my immune system had become…it was settled. We were going to the concert.

"Meet me at will call, bring earplugs. It will be high energy with lots of young people, really fun and uplifting. It will be so good for you!! We should all have seats in the same area so I will see you on and off. God's gonna bless you!"

"Oh yes, God has blessed me for sure. Thanks again for being part of His process."

So one week after I delivered my thank you letter, my husband and I found ourselves at the Portland Memorial Coliseum with hundreds of other people waiting to get into this sold-out concert. After a short wait at will call, one of my friend's daughters came smiling up to us and handed us the two golden tickets.

The tickets had seats for us on the floor, five rows from the end of the stage. The house lights went out, the spot lights came on, the music turned up. We could feel the base air move through our clothing. My friend was right in front of us.

Mandisa took the stage. *"Good Morning,"* she danced as she sang another of her hit songs. In between songs, she said she loves to hear stories about how others have also been overcomers and how it blesses her. Then she rocked the house with *"You're an Overcomer"* and a handful of other songs. Towards the end of her last song, my friend turned and motioned to come with her. What?! Mandisa is still singing, I thought. But I followed her to the end of the row. She slapped a sticker on the edge of my jacket and grabbed my hand, leading me around the crowd to the backstage area. About that time applause erupted in the coliseum as Mandisa finished her final number and was coming off the stage towards us. However, she turned and went around the stage the opposite direction as the next performer took the stage.

"She's going the long way around. Come on."

We went the short way and met her in front of her dressing room.

"Are you Jeri?"

She knew my name?

"I wanted to meet you."

I wanted to meet her, too.

"Tell me about the Diamond Girl Story."

I told her the story, explaining the Dolls, what they mean and how they fit together. I also shared the Operating Room story and how her song played throughout the OR during my un-medicated procedure. We all laughed at the doctor's responses and thanked Jesus for bringing encouragement through a song.

She prayed for me.

My friend and I prayed for her. It's lonely being on the road.

Hugs as we parted, a quick picture snapped and an invitation to come back after intermission…

"I have some things I want to give you."

As my friend and I returned to the dressing room, the bells on my phone started ringing. I explained the *thankful reminder* and expressed my appreciation. In turn, she handed me an *Overcomer* t-shirt and opened a CD. As she handed me the signed souvenir, she hugged me again and echoed the inscription...

"Jeri, you're an Overcomer!"–

And inside...

"Fight on!!!" Mandisa

What amazing connections.

The night ended with a ticker tape parade, which is a whole other story.

Thank You, Jesus.

> **"You, dear children, are from God and have OVERCOME them, because the One who is in you is greater than the one who is in the world"** (1 JOHN 4:4 NIV).

Mandisa's Letter

February 11, 2014

Dear Mandisa,

Thank you for being an "Overcomer" and with the same encouragement you found in Christ – you have encouraged me and countless others! Thank you!!!

In 2012, I was diagnosed and began a battle with Multiple Myeloma (MM) – a blood cancer. We began praying and stomping. Praying for the healing, strength and Peace for the battle. Stomping/ crushing MM under our feet. Otherwise it was in my face and I could easily lose my focus. There were things to do, places to go, and people to love.

When "Overcomer" came out, the radio station I was listening to not only played your song, they also aired a "voice byte." You were sharing about being an "Overcomer" with your weight and also wanting to be an encouragement for Robin Roberts, who was going through a bone marrow transplant. Sometimes referred to as a Stem Cell Transplant (SCT).

I cried with a ray of hope because "nothing's really going right." Treatments had stopped being effective and the MM numbers were climbing. The doctors were suggesting a SCT for me.

So, in November of 2013, I was admitted to the hospital for the SCT. So many thoughts/emotions – but there was Peace!

"Whatever it is you may be going through I know He's not gonna let it get the best of you."

Thank You, Jesus.

When this journey began, God gave me a special "story" and a vision for the simple props to tell it...a set of 3 Russian Dolls...aka "The Dolls". (With the help of some loved ones we actually created these dolls.)

THE DIAMOMD GIRL STORY

1 – The Outside Girl – covered with Band-Aids, scars, patches, scratches...falling apart.

2. – The Glass Girl – covered with broken pieces of glass. God can make something beautiful out of our brokenness... but we need to give Him all of the pieces.

3. – The Diamond Girl – covered with "diamonds". Because of Jesus' death/crucifixion and resurrection, she is healed, whole and forgiven...nothing can touch the Diamond Girl. She is heaven bound!!! (The unseen lasts)

This is the basic story. However, it is embellished as it is told.

Before I could check into my medical hotel room, I had a short procedure in the OR (Operating Room). The OR nurse, after hearing the "Diamond Girl Story," changed the radio station. The doctors didn't notice...at first. I was draped in a blue paper tent and told to turn away from the procedure. They used local numbing medicine, so I was very aware of the process! At one point the doctors were discussing the procedure and how to secure the device. Then one of them asked, "Who turned on that station?" Their hard rock music, that normally goes unnoticed by patients under general anesthetic, was missing! I'm not sure which local Christian station the nurse had found, but over the airwaves – "You're an Overcomer" came singing over me. "You might be down for a moment, feeling like it's hopeless" ...oh He reminded me through your song...He was "holding me right now." Thank You, Jesus, for the encouragement and the distraction. I wiped away more tears. I even told the doctors who you are!!! I found out later that the OR nurse thought I would appreciate the change in stations...she was right!

I believe there is a "Diamond Girl" or, for the guys, a "Diamond Guy" in each of us. Thank you for shining and being part of the process God is bringing me through! Press on Diamond Girl! Jesus Loves YOU!!

I'm in Good Hands,
Jeri Houle

✉ Sent: Friday, March 7, 2014

✉ Subject: Next Chapter 3-7-14 Landmark/Day +100

Hello again Stomping Team!

We passed a "Landmark" this last week: Day +100. In SCT (Stem Cell Transplant) "calendar language" that's a significant event. Lots of restrictions lifted, re-immunizations begin to boost the crippled immune system, gloved gardening can resume, and flowers and plants can come back into the house. I can do pretty much whatever I feel like doing. Naps are still good, but I'm getting stronger every day.

Bottom Line: Watch the trends, "blood counts are all pretty steady," continue maintenance treatment every other week.

This anticipated landmark was met with surprises. In addition to the flocks of singing robins in the trees and blooming daffodils, was a set of tickets to a concert and a coliseum filled with singing, praising and honoring Jesus. Mandisa, one of the performers, sings a song, *Overcomer,* which has been extremely encouraging during this SCT battle. Long story short, she heard about my *His-story* and asked to meet me back stage. So, with my ticket-giving-friend and a backstage pass, we spent about 10 minutes with a fellow "Overcomer." What a sweet lady. In the final minutes of the concert, our "stage-close" seats were showered with confetti.

Jesus reminded me that the ticker-tape parade was a celebration of overcoming the SCT battle. There's still a war to fight, but today, this season, it's time to celebrate, live life, and give thanks! God is so good!

I am thankful for family time-all together, beach trips, quarter-century birthday celebrations, "post" b-day chocolate cupcakes, Christmas in March, birds in puddle-bath-splashes, flower spotting, peeking blue sky, dinners with friends, mailbox surprises, writing time, breakthrough, ah-ha moments, messages, extremely short hair + hats, returning organized thoughts, 100-day-photo-journal, supportive family and friends, sharing the *Diamond Girl Story*, living life and knowing I'm...

In Good Hands,

Jeri

Thanks for listening.

✉ Sent: Monday, April 28, 2014

✉ Subject: Next Chapter 4-28-14 New Life/Remission Holding Steady

Happy Easter/Resurrection* Season to my Stomping Team!

I haven't stopped thinking of you and being thankful for the many ways I've been supported in this journey.

Bottom Line: Remission is holding steady! The ratio is improving. (The ratio of Kappa Light Chains/Multiple Myeloma to Lambda Light Chains.

We saw Dr. Onc (Oncology) this week. He is pleased with the improving Kappa/Lambda ratio. It means that my system continues to recover from the Stem Cell Transplant. My Creatinine (kidney function) is also holding under 2.0 and will most likely improve even more after the six-month mark, in May, when another medication is stopped.

Good Blood counts returning from "unmeasurable" during SCT to normal-ish, hair growing from bald to 1/2 inch, energy returning from horizontal to vertical, immune system fought off aches and fever without antibiotics; revival.

There is rejoicing.

The song birds are singing, the early spring flowers are blooming, leaves on the trees are unfolding, blades of grass are pushing through the dead leaves...there is an exhilarating rush of new life everywhere.

*Resurrection: the act of rising from the dead; a rising again, as from decay, disuse; revival.

Resurrection takes on a whole new level of meaning after coming through the depths of a Stem Cell Transplant (SCT). Easter shows up on the calendar and we are reminded that Jesus came back to life from death. There is rejoicing. The same Power that raised Jesus from the dead lives in me. He died to give me life, a life that will last forever.

I am in Good Hands,

Jeri

Resurrected Life

Looking at the Stem Cell Transplant process, it is amazing to see how it all parallels the life, death, and resurrection of Jesus. In a mysterious kind of way, I took great comfort knowing that as the life I had known literally came to a "death," that after some time there would be a "resurrected life" that slowly returned.

Jesus had resurrected life in three days.

They say SCT is about a 100-day process, gaining 1% strength each day. And then regaining muscle strength and stamina over the next year. Resulting in a *new normal.*

Because the blood counts went so immeasurably low from the massive chemo, I hung onto a thread of life. My immune system was wiped out along with much of the Myeloma.

I was very weak and tired.

I was in a "bubble of protection."

I was held together.

It was one of the closest places to physical death on this side of heaven.

After the three-week stay in the hospital, I was released to the safety of my home and my caring husband and family.

And in time, my physical strength returned.

And with the same Power living in me, that resurrected Jesus from death, I have a *resurrected life.*

...I want to know Christ, and the power of his resurrection and fellowship of his sufferings,

> becoming conformed to his death; in order
> that I may attain to the resurrection from the
> dead (PHILIPPIANS 3:10-11 NIV/NASB).

Because of the Cross, because of Jesus, I am held together and I live!

> And He (Jesus) is the image of the invisible
> God, the firstborn of all creation. For in Him
> all things were created, both in the heaven and
> on earth, visible and invisible, whether thrones
> or dominions or rulers or authorities; all things
> have been created through Him and for Him.
> And He is before all things, and in Him all
> things hold together (COLOSSIANS 1:15-17 NASB).

We are held together...one cell to another, by the cross of Jesus because of what He did in His death. But also in the way He created us and can hold us together.

I'm in Good Hands...holding me together...even if it does look like it's falling apart.

I know I am repeating myself here, but it's a good thing to think about again.

Just pondering...

Metamorphosis

Hibernation

Migration

Molting

Seasons

Life

Cycles...changes...transformations...all of creation created to mirror the life, death AND resurrected life of Jesus.

Life of a butterfly: Freedom, isolation, rest, FLIGHT

Life of a bear, squirrel, rabbit: Roaming, darkness, still, AWAKE

Life of a bird: Flying, distant, relocates, RETURN

Life of an eagle: Perched, separation, molt, SOAR

Life of a flower: Bloom, wither, dormant, NEW LIFE

The Bible says we are to identify ourselves with the death of Jesus AND His resurrected life <u>symbolically</u> through baptism. *

The process of Stem Cell Transplant is ONE of THE closest things to <u>actual</u> death on this side of Heaven AND planned resurrected life. I moved from my freedom, roaming, blooming life to one of isolation, darkness, and separation. I was relocated, withered, molted, still and restful for a season...but I have awakened, returned, re-bloomed, taken flight, soaring with NEW LIFE and an expanded appreciation for what my Lord has done for me, how much He loves me and is always there. Thank You, Jesus.

> *Therefore we have been buried with Him through baptism into death, so that as Christ was raised from the dead through the glory of the Father, so we too might walk in newness of life. For if we have become united with Him in the likeness of His death, certainly we shall be also in the likeness of His resurrection (ROMANS 6:4 NASB).

Paradise Promises!

Heavenly Sunset Hugs

Honeymoon[2]
Nepali Coast Line

LOVE

Paradise Birds And Flowers!

Paradise
Threatened

Pineapple Plantation

Storm Warnings!

Keep Telling *His-Story!*

Pearl Harbor

SECTION 9: SUMMER 2014

Paradise

Journey Goes On

More than two years have passed since this journey was started. And it's not ending here. The Lord has taken us from the Grand Canyon and the dark slimy pits of cancer to Hawaii and the paradise of remission. I have gone from the *white water rafting lessons* of "hold on tight and suck rubber" to the *stand up paddle lesson* of "keep balanced and if you fall, fall. Just get back up and go again." What a journey.

My husband told me that he'd always wanted to take me to Hawaii. So when I had suggested Disneyland, years ago for our honeymoon, he put Hawaii on hold. But now with my remission status, returning strength, lifted food restrictions, and his charge: "Do not wait until we retire," we were free to move about the cabin.

He said, "You're feeling good, so let's go."

Extra flight miles afforded our first class seats. A hot, flowered breakfast and hand towel awaited us in the sky. We were greeted with sunshine, blue skies, blue water, warm air, and tropical flowers. It was beautiful. It even smelled nice.

Our rental car allowed us to access the island at our own pace. We discovered one-lane bridges, tunnels of trees, gangs of chickens that really don't know when to crow, and beautiful flowers. Many, we had never seen. The blue ocean was inviting and thankfully warmer than our Oregon waters, which made snorkeling much more pleasant.

The catamaran, turned sailboat, gave us a view of the beautiful, accordion-like Nepali Coast line. We skimmed along the water with the dolphins, flying fish, and sea turtles.

Our condo was right on the beach next to the water. So even while resting, we could hear the surf and the meals on the lanai were a picnic.

Paradise.

We learned that pineapples grow on the ground, bananas grow upside down in huge clusters in a tree, and macadamia nuts are extremely hard to get out of their shells. Lemon, lime, mango, papaya, and coconut trees are used in landscaping. Many of the bushes and trees have a fragrant bloom. And while many of the plants do have a dormant season, not everything goes dormant at the same time. The flowers used in making leis grow abundantly, even in the wild.

Paradise.

There was a relaxed, calm that was allowing us both to enjoy each other and life around us. We rested when we needed to, went for walks, swims, snorkels and just sat, soaking it all in. We weren't in a hurry and plodded along when we were ready.

With a renewed sense of adventure, we drove around the island. Fresh markets and food trucks became a source of entertainment and nutrition.

There were so many beautiful things to see.

The adventure continued with kayaking up a river, then hiking into a secret waterfall. Thankfully, swift streams followed the knee-deep mud portions of the trail, so we could rinse off. That red dirt made its mark, though.

Another adventure took us out into the sea, beyond the breakers. We were on stand-up paddleboards. We were told to push off from shore, slip up onto the board on our stomach, then to our knees, and finally to stand. Our feet should be shoulder width apart, knees at ease to keep balanced. If we felt like we were going to fall, fall. And fall away from the board to avoid hitting it, because that would hurt. Easier said than done.

The push off the shore was met with deceivingly small, yet very powerful ocean waves. I tumbled with my board in the surf. Wasn't quite sure which way was up for a moment. Our instructor helped get me launched. And once I got past the shoreline, things went much more smoothly. Out in the sea, it was quiet and peaceful as we paddled up the coast. Surfers were trying to catch a wave between us and land. There was even a sea turtle that poked its head up and watched us pass by. And although we could see cars whiz by in the distance, life slowed down out there off shore.

Throughout our island journey I kept thinking this is a glimpse of paradise. And while it was very beautiful and full of adventure, it wasn't perfect.

It isn't the paradise I long for. We heard of storm warnings during our stay, even a hurricane watch and torrential rains after we left. There was an underlying current that we didn't belong there. We were constantly protecting ourselves from sunburn, wild drivers, and chicken poop. We swam with one eye open to the fact that there could have been sharks in the waters where we were playing. And Pearl Harbor gave sobering evidence of great conflict and loss.

Paradise on earth is threatened.

However, I believe there is a Paradise that is NOT being threatened. A place that is being prepared for me, where I do belong and all are welcome. There is a banqueting table where I will feast and the waves of His love will never stop washing over me, calling me deeper. It is a place where I will be completely healthy and safe in His Good Hands. I experience glimpses of that now, here on earth, and pray for His Kingdom to come and His will to be done. But this life is only a temporary situation, a sneak preview. It points to the Hope I have for the future. Paradise everlasting.

Waiting in the airport terminal, on our way home, we spotted a "Pizza My Heart" sign that summed up a lot of things. The response...

"You have the whole thing!"

In the mean time, there may be pits and canyons, storms, rainbows and clearing skies, waves and paradise...but it's only temporary.

One day I will trade it all in for an eternity in Paradise. I'm just passing through!

Holding on to His promises!

📧 Sent: Saturday, July 5, 2014

📧 Subject: Next Chapter 7-5-14 Fireworks/Chemo Fire Success

Greetings Stomping Friends,

July always has a variety of sparkles, whistles, and amazing colors along with loud booms and over-head bursts ... Fireworks!!!

It's part of the celebration for **freedom**, **independence** and **liberty**. Yes I know it's for the country, but in my own little world there is a celebration... "fire works."

Bottom line: The fire of chemo therapy/stem cell transplant is holding steady...even with a month off of maintenance treatment. And for the first time in years, all my CBC* blood tests are in the normal range. Thank You, Jesus.

(*CBC includes: white, red, hemoglobin, platelets, calcium, etc.)

Dr. Onc gave me some **freedom** last month: time off for an amazing anniversary/birthday trip to Hawaii with my husband. Freedom to "live my life!"

Independence has come since we "graduated" to every other month doctor visits and maintenance treatment every other week. (Instead of 2x/week during regular treatment.)

Eating fresh fruits and veggies at **liberty** is something I continue to enjoy and "playing" in the yard with all the soil and the flowers, is also a treat. (Oh yes weeds, too. I don't enjoy the weeds as much as the flowers, but it's a good reminder that there will always be things that need to be pulled out of my life.)

Dr. Onc was very pleased this week with the CBC tests, Kappa Light Chain (Multiple Myeloma) and Creatinine (kidney function). It will be interesting to see if there will be an improvement in the numbers now that we are back to the maintenance treatment. But holding steady and living life is a great combo!

Celebrating 29 married years and 52 years of life, healthy kids, sunsets and sunrises over the sea, fresh fruit, mud paths to waterfalls, turtles, dolphins, up-close fish, balance for SUP paddling, smooth flights, 1st's-classy, snorkeling, surf, trade winds, cards, texts, phone calls, Mac-nuts, "short-limo" service, timely messages, and fire-shows.

The Bible describes God as a "Consuming Fire"...whether He's lighting up the night or burning out the impurities, Fire Works.

In Good Hands,
Jeri

Fiery Furnace · Looking Back

Thankfully, I have never been in an actual fire. However, I have burned things, been near a blazing fire, felt its heat, and seen what little remains when it is finally extinguished.

During a family vacation to the Oregon coast, we spent an afternoon at a glass blowing shop. The craftsmen individually guided each of us through the process of creating a colorful glass float. The glowing hot furnace, also known as the glory hole, contained a vat of molting-hot liquid glass. A very long, pipe-like rod was dipped into the vat and with a steady rolling motion, a scorching blob of glass was brought out. Moving quickly, the glass blob was rolled onto a metal table, covered with little piles of broken, colored pieces of glass. Once the surface of the glass blob was covered in the broken pieces the whole ensemble, still rolling, was put back into the furnace. The constant rolling motion kept the blob of glass from dripping off the rod. Thankfully there was a heat shield to stand behind so the hair on our arms didn't get singed too badly. It was toasty.

At one point the blob of glass was brought out and long-handled, oversized tweezers were pushed into the colored streaks and twisted, creating swirls of color in the sphere.

Working quickly, then back into the heat, rolling constantly. Eventually, the hot ball was shaped with a wooden form. Then air was blown into the cool tip of the rod, filling and expanding the intensely hot blob of glass, enlarging it to the desired size. The experts did some finishing touches, cut the glass float away from the rod, and then laid each sphere in a covered box to cool over night. If cooled too quickly the glass float could shatter, sending shards of colored glass everywhere. We came back the next day to retrieve our *something beautiful* made from the broken pieces.

This medical journey has been described as a fiery furnace, and I must say the fire got plenty hot. During a fire like this, some things just don't matter. Other things are burned away. Yes, my body went through it's own refining and the bad blood was burned away giving way to new healthy blood. But my heart also went through a refining fire. I like to think of the glass girl going into the furnace of God's love. Many things get burned away and yet the precious things in my heart get purified and revealed. Broken pieces of attitudes, wooden bad choices, straw doubts, hay hurts, un-forgiveness, and jealousies give way to the gold truth, priceless forgiveness, gems of sight, love, acceptance, patience, and renewed motivations.

And while no one can be in the fiery furnace with me, I have come to realize that Jesus has been there all along. And He's making something beautiful out of all those broken pieces.

> **Now if any man builds upon the foundation with gold, silver, precious stones, wood, hay, straw, each man's work will become evident; for the day will show it because it is to be revealed with fire, and the fire itself will test the quality of each man's work** (1 Corinthians 3:12 NASB).

Something Beautiful

There is a story within the story, an inside story. It's an invisible transformation that God has worked through suffering and hard times. I think about the story a lot. The Dolls help tell *His-Story* of Hope. I hear the story when I tell it. The Outside Girl is falling apart. The Glass Girl is being made beautiful because all the broken pieces are being given to Jesus. And The Diamond Girl continues to learn the Real Truth that is changing everything. The Diamond Girl reflects the Light that shines from God.

I carry the Dolls in a little black bag tucked away inside my purse, along with a little turquoise bag for the diamond beads. When I tell the story, I share a diamond bead. It's not about the bead; it's about the diamond inside.

It's about allowing God to have ALL the broken pieces and trusting Him to keep me in Good Hands.

Really Lord, ALL of the broken pieces?

Some things are embarrassing.

What will they think?

Yes, I want them all.

I know about each of the pieces.

It doesn't matter what they think. It matters what I think.

I AM putting all the pieces together to make something beautiful.

You do not realize now what I am doing but later you will understand (John 13:7 NIV).

I have tried to stay away from telling this piece of my story. But, alas, when I tell God He can use my life, at some point I must surrender and actually give it all to Him.

You can have my broken pieces Lord.

I'll take good care of all that you give Me.

I won't embarrass you.

The important thing is that you let Me have them.

I know the details. They don't need all of the details.

I've told the Diamond Girl Story A LOT!

What I've come to realize is I HAVE NEEDED TO HEAR it. God could have instantly, miraculously healed the blood cancer, my physical ailment. But He knew what it would take in order to be healed from all the broken pieces of my inward parts, IF I would let Him have all the pieces. The glass girl was full of an unseen, very real *dis-ease*.

And He knew that.

From a very early age I remember my Mom called me a "worry wart" and said I asked a lot of questions.

Am I going to be ok?

Do I really have to stay in my own room, alone?

I did what I could to have everyone like me and say I was a "good girl." I was very helpful. I listened to the adult conversations to see if they said anything good about me.

Did they approve?

Did I do it good enough?

And if I did it good enough, maybe I should do it better next time?

I was afraid of fire and had nightmares about our house burning down. I also didn't like walking behind the neighbor's truck because I thought a lion would come out and attack me.

Is there anybody here to protect me?

Am I safe?

Going to the doctor would cause me to vomit, even if I didn't have the flu. I got sick on the first day of school every year in grade school. But I worked hard and got good grades.

Do they approve of me now?

If I put on a happy face and a little skip to my step maybe they wouldn't notice I was really missing my dad and hoping he would come live with us again. The principal called home. He told my mom he was concerned that I didn't have any friends and was very shy. He saw through my disguise. But with all his other responsibilities, I was forgotten and went back to my charades.

Does anyone really see me?

Am I fitting in?

"Lets try counseling."

So one day, during elementary school, Mom took me to a counselor. We talked about getting sick when I went to the doctors office and the first day of school, for no apparent reason. The strange lady had me draw a picture of the doctor. He was lopsided in my drawing and she thought **I didn't have the right**

perspective of the people who were trying to help me. Maybe she was right.

Do I see clearly?

Can I try hard enough to get it right?

Mom also took me to the fire department. The firemen gave us a tour of all the equipment and a home evaluation to see if we lived in a safe house. It all looked good.

Am I safe?

Is there an escape if I need it?

I found pieces in my life that were broken from *way back*. But even now as I write these things out, more of the pieces are coming together. Thank you, Jesus!

I was a leader in High School and strived to say "hi" to everyone and cheer them on. Yet, I walked through the empty, darkened gymnasium to avoid the hallway full of people.

Am I good enough?

What do they think of me?

I had too many boy friends and mistrusted too many girl friends. There was a hole in my heart.

Who would fill it?

Am I pretty?

Do I have what it takes?

Do they like me?

Did I upset them?

I was doubled over in pain when Mom took me to the doctor. It wasn't appendicitis like we thought. He told me I had a bad case of stress and needed to "talk" to someone. **Keeping uncomfortable thoughts and feelings bottled up inside would eventually cause physical things to go wrong. Maybe doctors**

could be helpful. Oh, that stress? I was working a summer job in a city office.

Am I doing it right?

Do I meet your expectations?

Do you like me?

At the same time I had another boyfriend. He was an older high school guy. My parents did not approve. I didn't want to break up with the guy, yet I wanted to please them.

Do you love me?

Do you have time for me?

Am I important?

Do I matter?

Can I MAKE you pay attention to me?

I think I was underhandedly rebellious. But thankfully, we all survived those years!

In college I tried to be the counselor to a young woman who came into my room to talk and then I realized she was delusional, suicidal, and out of control. Oh, I didn't handle that well. Tried to find comfort and consoling for myself after that evening.

Do I have what it takes?

Am I in the right place?

That situation added to my doubt. I really didn't have what it takes. Funny, now that I think about it, just before I graduated from college, my supervising teacher asked me if I ever thought about being a counselor. **Maybe she saw something I didn't see.**

Married life looked good from a distance and on the surface. But I knew, on the inside, it was stressful when my gut started aching again. I didn't want to cause any waves.

Do you really love me?

Can you see that I'm hurting, too?

Do I matter?

My husband and I built walls, clammed up, and didn't want to get hurt. I wanted a partner to live life with, not to battle. The more I asked about making a plan for events or outings, the further away he retreated. Finally he said "Just go ahead and do whatever, I'm not going." I ran, literally, for miles at a time. It was a lonely time. I was vulnerable and unprotected.

Do you want to be with me?

Am I good enough?

Do you know I love you?

Where do I fit in your life? Do I?

I chose to love him, but I didn't know if he was getting the message. He had his own issues. I asked for some advice from another married couple. That was fine until she didn't want to meet anymore and it was just her husband and me chatting. DANGEROUS!!! Thankfully that got halted before too much damage had been done. But it was a breaking point.

Can this be fixed?

Would we both be willing to work on this marriage?

Are we done?

We would work on it!!!

We tried going together to get some help, which I believe was the right move. I heard a few things that were helpful. "Your marriage is like a garden, it needs to be weeded and maintained." The pastor also talked about how words get twisted. What I speak from my mouth wasn't necessarily what my husband heard. That explained a lot about our misunderstandings. And saying it louder didn't help. He challenged us to help the other become the best version of ourselves we could be. That would be a lifetime project if we made it through this bump in the road. Finally, I heard the "list" that my husband kept in his head, all the time, of things he was doing already for our family. I was only frustrating him more when I asked him to help me with my list. I had no idea. But, he was done with counseling.

So I found a counselor for me. I went in with the idea that I could fix my husband. I was quickly redirected, I left him in God's Hands and we began to work on me.

Who am I?

Who does God say I am?

What does it mean to be whole?

Oh, there were way more broken pieces than I realized.

I still thought it was my husband that needed to be fixed, but I worked on my stuff.

I started stuffing difficult thoughts and feelings again, just like in high school. I recognized it this time, but went to the doctor any way. After hearing my life woes, the doctor called me a "hero." Wow. **He actually validated me and all the stuff I'd been through.** Said there should be a ticker-tape parade for me. God took care of that one.

Somewhere in all of this I started going to church again and really **listening with my heart.** I remember sitting in the pew, with the music playing, sobbing as I heard about how much Jesus loves me, how He understands the broken parts of me, and reminded me I wasn't alone. In those days, I sat next to a dear older lady, who, for weeks, would put her arms around me at just the right moment, give me a hug and hand me Kleenex. I learned about the **Great Counselor Who knows everything about me and knows exactly what I need. I really was in Good Hands.**

If He can see everything about me, isn't He disappointed?

Can I work hard enough to earn His approval?

Can I do enough so He won't leave me?

If I keep busy, maybe I can avoid the hurts.

In church I learned how I had been adopted into a heavenly family and that my Father would never leave me. Huge piece!

Would He REALLY stay with me?

Can I really trust Him?

I also learned of a woman who was caught in adultery and brought to Jesus. He forgave her. Later He said because she has been forgiven much, she loves much. And she washed His feet with her hair and tears. The story was told to me in pantomime.

Could I really be forgiven of all my wrong?

Can I love Him with everything I have?

How can I love Him and my husband?

There was an amazing friend that came into my life that listened and validated me. We would share the ups and downs of life together and challenged each other to "jump" into whatever God had set up for us next. She listened and encouraged me to hang in there. We "sharpened iron." But I still had my doubts.

Is she going to tell others about my struggles?

Will she betray me?

This seems too good too be true?

My husband and I got brave and attended a weekend marriage conference. They even talked about the walls that couples build up and how to tear them down. We were on the right track. The speaker said my spouse was God's perfect gift for me. Hmmm. God would have to help me see it, but I was willing to learn to appreciate and choose to love even when it was hard. Some days it felt like we were both putting water in a bucket with holes.

Is this working?

Am I making a difference?

Are things really changing?

What else can I do?

This is so hard.

Can I just come *home* to be with You?

A few years prior to the diagnosis, there was another very challenging, shattering season. There were deaths in the family, kids graduating and moving, working an opposite schedule as my husband and some very poor choices. We pulled back from each other again and had gone into survival mode. Beyond some miscommunication, depression, and disregard at home, my decision to share some of my frustration with the wrong person was not a good choice. It shattered the trust my husband and I had built up.

Will he ever trust me again?

Does he want to keep me?

Does he love me?

Am I good enough?

Does he really want me?

Is he going to leave physically now, too?

Does he really want to live life together?

Is there something wrong with me?

Am I a priority?

My husband will tell you he should have been protecting me. I will tell you I should not have been talking to a male someone about the things at home. But we could be *shoulding* ourselves all day. It became a tangled mess. We were both wrong and it almost cost us our marriage. I left my job and came home to rest and take care of my family. I remember saying, *"What ever it takes"* to the Lord to save my marriage and have it flourish.

We saw a counselor together this time. She was very clear and very direct.

To my husband, "Do you want this marriage?" "Yes!"

To me, "Do you want this marriage?" "Yes"

Double yes!

We told her about a terrible car accident that our daughter and both of us had been in on Valentines weekend. A big 350 truck lost control on a slippery freeway going about 65 mph. The truck hit the driver-side, backseat passenger door of our little car, opposite of our daughter. I turned when I heard the terror in our daughters scream only to see the grill of this truck making impact to our car and the glass of the window shatter all over our precious cargo. I joined her scream.

My husband kept saying, "We're going to be all right. The car is doing its job. We're going to be alright."

I kept thinking this is going to hurt. Is it ever going to stop?

We were in slow motion.

Our car spun and finally came to rest in the middle of the freeway headed the direction we had just come from. We were able get the car pulled off to the side, but the truck continued to move and flipped over a full rotation. It was all very scary. Thankfully, other than some very sore muscles and the emotional trauma, everyone, including the truck passengers, walked away. Thank you, Jesus!

After hearing the story the counselor said of my husband,

"Here is your coverage."

"He is your protector."

"You need to rest. There is a little girl inside of you that needs to know she is truly loved. And she needs to know how to play. Go home and plant a flower."

She also told us to read a book (Dr. O). We were learning to take responsibility for our self and for our own emotions and learning to **ask** for what we need from the other. We were both willing to work on it.

A few more broken pieces were coming together.

This same counselor gave me a couple of other assignments. I was to attend a counselor training session and just be there to soak up the information.

She also asked, "How would you like to help me write a children's book?"

She was nudging me into a place I needed to be. She didn't know that my husband had always said I could write children's books. So, I was going to help her write a children's book. Which we did the following summer in cooperation with a team of adults and children. It was fantastic. I learned I had a "voice."

The counselor training session allowed me to see other people who also had broken pieces. But they were being put back together and helped each other with the brokenness. They practiced counseling with each other. During one session I volunteered to be the counselee. I was full of shame and very broken by the unfaithful patterns in my life towards my husband. They mapped highlights of my life journey including the divorce of my parents and the empty space I had with Dad being away from me. I held the notebook over my face and hid in shame with tears streaming down my face as I tried to answer their questions.

"It wasn't your fault."

Adult decisions didn't have anything to do with me, yet I had carried that responsibility and the consequences of their choice! I had learned that pattern well and that day it began to break off! **Some things need to break before they can be whole.** Overall in life, having a wise and caring friend who listens to my stories and encourages me through it all, is priceless. Sometimes just *talking it out* helps me hear myself. I can hear how off base I am and other times things just start to make sense and the pieces come together. Having another perspective is helpful. It's not a fix-it session, more like validation, someone to help find the good in things when the good is hard to find.

The spring prior to the diagnosis, my husband and I attended another marriage conference. The pastors challenged us in some areas. They asked us to grade our spouse and ourselves. We both came away with better grades than we expected and we were encouraged to work on improving some weak areas. We were to remember:

"He's a good man with a good heart and he loves me.
I am a good woman with a good heart and I love him."
(Eggerich)

Another very key piece of advice:

"Don't wait until you retire to do the things you want to do.
Treat your wife like a queen."

Really? A queen?

I'm not Cinderella in the corner in my own little world?

Was my prince really on his way to me?

Soon after this conference, we booked a trip of a lifetime. Grand Canyon here we come. My husband had heard my heart. What an amazing, healing time. Laughter is good medicine.

Yes, more pieces are coming together, for us both.

We've come to realize that in our marriage we are two broken people on a journey and our paths have crossed. **The goal, to**

become the best version of me I can be and support him, as he becomes the best version of him he can be while supporting me. Which really means, I still have stuff to work on. He can't fix me!!! I can't fix him!!! But he has shown me unconditional love through it all and I've seen the way he looks at me. My husband loves me!

The Great Counselor continues to put pieces together. And many times it involves other people that bring a message.

For many years, I have had a very wise friend who will call me out of the blue and listen. Listen. Among other things, she noticed how busy I was, distracted, running, and preoccupied on other things. She modeled "intense quietness," being "Father-tuned." Tuned into what my Father had to say.

Can I really learn to "be still and know" He is God?

Does the hurt really build my capacity for joy?

Will I really have what it takes when I need it? I can't store it up?

Does being thankful really change things?

She had endearing names for me. She and her husband have embraced me at pivotal times. I felt cherished.

When the cancer diagnosis was being sorted out, I contacted a counselor/mentor friend and asked her some questions. I knew that physical aliments could result from emotional baggage.

What kinds of physical aliments cause blood cancer?

What kinds of physical aliments cause kidney *dis-ease*?

She added, "What are the spiritual roots?"

We dove in.

In the Bible it says:

Gloom and doom leave you bone-tired.

Said another way:

A broken spirit dries up the bones (PROVERBS
17:22B MSG/NASB).

She asked me some questions:

"What's in the bones?"

"Bone marrow."

"What does that produce?"

"Red/white blood cells"

*"If your immune system is compromised we always go back
to 'Who broke your heart?' Also part of the root is rejection,
especially from a father."*

Hmmmmm! I knew I missed a relationship with Dad. I'd
worked on a few layers of this before. Healing childhood wounds,
having a "father's blessing" prayed over me, having an adopted
father figure, forgiving Dad, and building a relationship with
him, to name a few. **In my head I knew all my parental figures
did the best they could and they really did love me. But there
were still some broken pieces that needed to be put together.**

She asked me more questions:

Do you know your heavenly Father adores you?

You are precious in His sight!

*Do you know that He is devoted to you and wants to see you
succeed?*

Do you know you haven't disappointed Him?

Do you understand His affection for you?

*Do you feel His embrace? He participates in the hug. You are
HELD!*

Do you know He says you're good enough?

NOPE, not completely…more broken pieces coming to the surface.

I knew these things were true, in my head, but my heart didn't seem to retain this important information. There really was a hole in my bucket. My friend said we were going to find a way to cement this important truth into my bucket.

My view of God continued to change. She reminded me that I was fearfully and wonderfully made and asked me even more questions.

"Besides your blood, what else isn't working correctly?"

"My kidneys."

"What is the kidney's function?"

"The body's filter system, they help remove waste from the body. Mine are *clogged.*"

My filtering system was another piece of my *dis-ease.* Yes my kidneys were the physical part that wasn't working correctly, but also my mental, emotional, and spiritual filtering systems weren't working correctly either. Here were even more broken pieces. I needed to start filtering everything through God and what He said. What He said was and is true. His words trumped my belief of the truth or more accurately, the lies I had been holding on to.

We worked to break off the "strongholds" that had been attached to me. I took responsibility for the wrong things I had done and that had been done to me. I thought and felt at a deeper, more honest level. More of the questions that I had been asking throughout my life were being reinserted as positive statements.

My heavenly Father adores me.

I am precious in His sight.

He is devoted to me and wants to see me succeed.

He really does love me…really.

He holds me in Good Hands.

He says I am good enough…just the way I am. And invites me to grow.

Yes a cheerful disposition is good for your health. Said another way: **A joyful heart is good medicine** (PROVERBS 17:22A MSG/NASB).

To say that this cancer battle rocked our world would be an understatement. But God really did know how to use this shake-up to realign the broken pieces of both of our lives.

I'll never forget the trouble, the utter lost-ness, the taste of ashes, the poison I've swallowed. I remember it all - oh, how well I remember - the feeling of hitting the bottom. But there's one other thing I remember, and remembering, I keep a grip on hope (LAMENTATIONS 3:19-21MSG).

When life is heavy and hard to take, go off by yourself. Enter the silence. Bow in prayer. Don't ask questions: wait for hope to appear. Don't run from trouble. Take it full-face. The worst is never the worst (LAMENTATIONS 3:28-30 MSG).

I called out your name, O God, called from the bottom of the pit. You listened when I called out, "Don't shut your ears! Get me out of here! Save me!" You came close when I called out. You said, "It's going to be all right" (LAMENTATIONS 3:55-57 MSG).

More positive statements have emerged and are making their way from my head into my heart:

Perseveres with Joy.

God likes me!

He enjoys being with me!

He has forgiven me.

He makes me whole.

He's given me fortitude…a mental and emotional strength in facing difficulty, adversity, danger, or temptation courageously.

I am the King's daughter.

I am beautiful.

I am His prize.

I am important.

I was created for a purpose.

I am unique.

He won't betray me.

I can trust Him.

I am safe.

I am loved.

I am cherished.

I am treasured.

I am good enough!

God is making something beautiful out of my brokenness. And another beautiful part is that I have a husband who affirms these things with his words and actions. He likes being with me and I like being with him. I know I am a priority, even if there are times he isn't right beside me. He is committed to our family. His role of protecting, providing, praying, and playing are cemented into place. There may be cracks from where things were broken and still some places to mend. But God has made something beautiful out of our brokenness and we are a work in process. Together, we have stuck it out. I know my husband is not the enemy. But we have an enemy that would like to destroy us and has almost succeeded on a number of occasions. We have learned to ask questions to understand what is being said.

Is this what you meant when you said <abc>?

No I meant <xyz>!

Oh, you meant <xyz>?

Yes, that's right <xyz>!

We also understand that we think differently.

"He has blue thoughts, sees with blue lenses and hears with blue hearing aides." "I have pink thoughts, see with pink lenses and hear with pink hearing aides."
(Eggerich)

He has a "waffle brain." There are little compartments or boxes that he can open and close and think inside, one at a time.

I have a "spaghetti brain." My thoughts can mix together from one thought to another.

"Quiet" doesn't mean he's thinking about something. It may be that he's enjoying just being together, like when we're shoulder to shoulder driving down the road or sitting watching a football game. Other times he's in his "nothing box" and is really thinking about absolutely nothing. I have learned to give him time to "close one box" before I ask him about something in another box.
Life is much more pleasant.
(Ferrel)

To help reassure me, my husband has learned to say, *"You haven't done anything wrong,"* before he asks me to clarify something. And instead of saying "You don't want to do that," because maybe I really do want to do "it," he'll let me know he is uncomfortable with the situation and he needs reassuring. When I start to slip back into doubts or self-criticism, he will say something like, *"Be careful how you talk about my wife,"* or *"Cut yourself some slack."* We are appreciating each other's gifts and complimenting the efforts. *"Thank you"* goes a long way when we are working together.

The way we talk to each other now is more like a coach encouraging the team. And that approach is a safe place for me. I can offer help and suggestions and I'm not intimidated, where before I was afraid of doing something wrong and went into hiding. Or, I was so frustrated because he wasn't getting up and doing anything. I could plan something and he would say, "I don't want all my time planned for me!" Yet, on the other hand he didn't want to be the event planner and plan an event. I couldn't win. We were both stuck.

However, we found a compromise. We made a list of things that we needed and wanted to do in a week. The list included chores, like cleaning house and laundry, mowing the lawn, bathing the dogs, and projects. It also included fun things like going to church, walks, bike rides, boat rides, picnics, volunteering, having company, and trying a new food cart. We made a tally mark next to the item that we accomplished and pushed a *"that was easy"* button.

We have tickets to another marriage conference. It just keeps getting better. My husband really is God's perfect gift for me. We balance each other. There is a diamond hidden inside each of us. We've become treasure hunters. We're not perfect; there are still broken pieces. However, as we walk through life's journeys, surrendering to God, more and more of the broken pieces of our lives are put back in place. My eyes are opened to seeing the beautiful work He is doing.

It truly is something beautiful.

I'm sure there will be much more written about these three

little wooden dolls. In the mean time, I know the *Outside Girl* is getting stronger and livin' life, even though the days are numbered. God gets to decide the number. The *Glass Girl* is being mended and the broken pieces put back together. Something beautiful is being made in the process. I will keep giving Him all the broken pieces and He will bring ease out of my *dis-ease*. And the *Diamond Girl* continues to get stronger, knowing and following the Truth.

To say that I've seen a counselor all my life is an accurate statement. I finally understand the Great Counselor is with me all the time. However, He allows others to help counsel me. So between the pastoral care, running teams, Bible study leaders, friends, family, husband, even strangers, the Great Counselor, the Holy Spirit, has been doing some amazing work putting the broken pieces back together to make something beautiful. I choose to cooperate. I am a work in the progress. It's good hard work. But it's so worth it.

Chocolate Chip Cookies

Some of my favorite lessons for learning about how much God loves me has come through chocolate chip cookies. (CCCookies) That's right, the reassuring sweetness of the comforting love of God, all wrapped up in cookies.

Cookies were always a treat growing up. Mom made the best. She taught my brother and I how to make CCCookies. Love poured through her gift. Later, we made cookies at our house, in my kitchen. Now our kids make them on their own. There is something special about them.

A few years ago, in the midst of walking with my Grandma to the gates of heaven, God reminded me that He was close and was comforting me. The CCCookie was part of His message.

When chemotherapy had started, fear was creeping in; doubts that God would even want to heal me racked my thinking. My weight was climbing, uncertainty about my future seized me, and I questioned if God even loved me. I must have done something terribly wrong to have this happening to me. I was shriveling up inside. I was broken. I cried. It was not a fun time.

During this crazy season, I wasn't driving. My friend came twice a week to pick me up. She took me to my husband's work so he and I could travel to my treatments together. She knew I had been in an emotional struggle. So one day when she pulled up to my house, she told me there was a surprise in the glove box. I love surprises. Warm CCCookies. I cried some more. But these

were happy tears. He sent my friend as His messenger.
He does love me.

Recently, when my husband and I returned to the mainland after an amazing paradise vacation, we had an overnight layover in California. On top of all the other wonderful ways I was loved on this trip, there were CCCookies at the desk when we checked into our hotel.

He loves me!

If love, acceptance, and approval were kept in a bucket, my once hole-filled bucket was getting cemented in and the message becoming permanent. My husband is also reinforcing the message. He will often say, "Have I told you I love you today?" We both understand hugs are given and received at the same time. So now instead of me lifting his arms up into a full embrace, he holds me close as long as I want.

He loves me!

✉ Sent: Tuesday, September 9, 2014

✉ Subject: Next Chapter 9-9-14 Keep Watching/Holding Steady

Hello Stomping Friends

Wow, already September. Fall is in the air here. Leaves are starting to dance to the ground, the geese are starting their "fly-by" drills and the sun is slipping lower into the sky. A "normal" turn of the seasons. There is always something changing, always something to keep watching.

In addition to the seasons, we keep watching my blood counts.

Bottom Line: Remission is holding steady!

Dr. Onc is pleased. Maintenance treatment will continue

every other week. AND new medications are being developed that could be helpful during my lifetime.

I've started keeping time by the major events in my life. August 2014 marked the two-year point of when this battle with Multiple Myeloma began. I also began sending out these updates. Some of you have been stomping/praying a long time. Thank you to all of you no matter how long. What an encouragement. In those early emails I talked about "celebrating...soon...tough things first." Meaning that some time soon there would be a celebration of victory over whatever was puzzling the doctors, but there might be some tough things to go through before the celebration began. Oh yes, that may have been an understatement!

And while I am celebrating the new normal, clearer thinking, "increasingly energized," water drinking, curly-haired life (Thank You, Jesus!), finding something to celebrate everyday, even in the hard days, is worth the effort. It may not change my situation, but my outlook is lifted. Gloom shifts. Hope rises. And no matter what the outcome, there is a Celebration!

Keep Watching!

I'm in Good Hands,

Jeri

✉ Sent: Wednesday, September 10, 2014
✉ Subject: Next Chapter 9-10-14 Curly Hair Proof/Life

Hello again,

Some of you have asked to see this new curly hair...here's proof!

And evidence of the adventure my husband and I went on this weekend! (The sun did break out later in the day!)

Livin' Life!

In Good Hands,

Jeri

September 7, 2014 - Columbia River @ Astoria, Oregon - Coho Salmon

---

✉ Sent: Friday, October 24, 2014
✉ Subject: Next Chapter 10-24-14

Hello my Stomping Friends,

Hope you are well. These emails are getting further apart.

Bottom Line: Remission is holding steady!

At my last appointment, Dr. Onc continues to be very pleased with the numbers. The Multiple Myeloma is responding to the maintenance treatment, dropping a couple points over the last month. There were discussions about all the childhood immunizations that needed to be replaced at the one-year Stem Cell Transplant anniversary, follow-up needed with Dr. OHSU, and a repeat bone marrow biopsy. Not fun! Dates were set on the calendar. I started Round 10 on the Maintenance Plan and left the building.

A few days later the coordinator called and said Dr. OHSU had been in, noticed how well I was doing based on the numbers, and cancelled both the follow up appointment AND the bone marrow biopsy. Whoohoo! Thank You, Jesus!

So medically speaking, things are going very well. Thank you so much for all your prayers, stomping, and support.

I have made an observation:

My story is unique in the fact that it has been in the forefront of my mind. (And yours, too, at times.) However the **pattern** of my story is not so unusual. I think recognizing the **pattern** and cooperating with the process helps my perspective. However, that doesn't necessarily mean that the situation has changed.

Jesus said in this life we all **will** have trials. I **will** find myself in the pits. Something hard, sad, frustrating, disappointing, etc. **will** happen again at some point along the way. The question for me now is, *"Will I use the **pattern** I learned during this cancer battle for the next dark time?"* I will attempt to review the basic **pattern** here; maybe it will help someone else. I know I need it.

In the pits:

Body is weak, tears flowing, gut aching, heart pounding.

Emotions are churning, anger rising, sadness overwhelming, fear crippling, heart breaking. How can I go on?

Spirit is squished, broken, crying out...Jesus Help!

On the Rock, dripping with mud:

Body is tired, needs rest, food, exercise. Deep sigh.

Emotions are fighting, *what-if*, *if-only*. Disbelief. Confusion. How could this happen? Why me? Find a way to be thankful. Find the good in things when good is hard to find. I set bell alarms to ring, reminding me to be thankful.

Spirit is rescued out of the pit and set on a Rock! Lift spiritual eyes up and beyond this situation. I'm in Good Hands.

Uncharted Path:

Body gets up and moves, muscles stiff, sluggish.

Emotions stomp on "it." Put "it" under my feet. Disbelief replaced with acceptance and lots of questions. Which way should I go now? How will I know what is right and true?

Spirit finds a promise to hold on to. Take Jesus' hand. Talk to Him like He can hear me. He is good and He loves me! I can trust Him.

Fog:

Body presses on, doesn't give up.

Emotions are out of focus, confusing, frustrated, guarded. Coming out sideways. Bring all the broken pieces to Jesus.

Spirit releases it, surrenders to Jesus. Put it on the "altar" and offer it as a sacrifice to the Lord. He's in control. This didn't surprise Him. *"Not my way, but Yours, Lord."*

Clear Skies:

Body takes deep breath and ease is restored.

Emotions settle, calm, relaxed. Joy and peace come in. There is breakthrough. That was tough, but I made it through.

Spirit is rejoicing, nothing in between God and me.

We all have a story. We all have **patterns**, some work, and some, not so much. Our stories are part of *His-story*. The question now is "Will we share it?"

Thanks for listening to my *His-story*. I'm working on writing it down. God has given me such a gift of Hope. I know this is something I get to share. My prayer is that the Hope I have found may go beyond me. That part is up to God. My part is to finish the project and then leave it in Good Hands!

I'm in Good Hands,

Jeri

P.S. I hope one day I can hear your story!

Surrounded With Songs!

Fear NOT!

Something Beautiful In the Making!

Faith

Fiery Furnace - HOT!

Praise Changes Things!

Keep Shining!

SECTION 10:

P.S. - Post Script

Song Interview

This writing project needs to come to a soft close. This writing needs to be finished. My life is NOT finished. The next chapter may not be written down in print, but my life will continue. At the moment my thoughts are scattered. I am sitting at a table with old journals, copies of the second rough draft that a couple friends marked up for me, sticky notes with miscellaneous ideas, pens, paper, and a computer.

I feel like I've hit a wall. Stopped, stuck, and unproductive.

You have been physically slowed down. But that's not a bad thing. I am with you. I am working in areas you haven't noticed yet. Continue to live today. Yes, I know what your tomorrows hold, but if you are worrying about the what-ifs and maybes, you're not living today to the fullest. Enjoy what I've given you today!

We're in this together. It's gonna be okay. Your honest, thankful heart is such a gift to me. Our writing time is a reminder of what I have told you, your foundations. Our pictures and analogies help make it solid. I will continue to give you inspiration. Wait for it!

I love you.

Enjoy your day.

-God

As I went back through the journals, little details started to pop out. These verses had created a safety net for me:

> *You are my hiding place; you will protect me from trouble and surround me with songs of deliverance (PSALMS 32:7 NIV).

> *Many are the woes of the wicked, but the Lord's unfailing love surrounds the man who trusts in Him (PSALMS 32:10 NIV).

> *Rejoice in the Lord and be glad, you righteous; sing, all you who are upright in heart! (PSALMS 32:11 NIV).

When these verses were first copied down, I was in the flurry of the major storm. The diagnosis and treatment options were being discussed. And while I like to sing, I couldn't find my singer voice. I realize now, there have been songs all around me during the entire journey.

I have captured some of the encouraging song lyrics in a mock interview. The song lyrics represent my answers to the questions or my thoughts about the question. (Most of the songs are found on contemporary Christian radio stations and I heard them on the journey.)

Questions and Song Answers:

1. What was your prayer during this battle?

Lord, I need You.

Oh, I need You.

Every hour I need You.

My one defense, my righteousness,

Oh God, how I need You.

Matt Maher/All The People Said Amen: Lord I Need You

2. What was it like facing the cancer diagnosis?

There's a wave that's crashing over me, and all I can do is surrender.

Whatever You're doing inside of me It feels like chaos, but somehow there's peace.

And it's hard to surrender to what I can't see, but I'm giving in to something heavenly.

Sanctus Real/We Need Each Other: Whatever You're Doing

3. With the diagnosis of cancer you must have had many thoughts of how horrible treatment would be and heard stories full of fear and dread. That must have been devastating.

(Yes!)

But the Voice of Truth tells me a different story.

The Voice of Truth says do not be afraid!

The Voice of Truth says this is for My glory!

Out of all the voices calling out to me,

I will choose to listen and believe the Voice of Truth.

Casting Crowns/Life Song: Voice of Truth

4. Where did your strength come from?

My source of strength

My source of hope

Is Christ alone!

Brian Littrell/In Christ Alone: In Christ Alone

5. What is a feathered hideout?

You are my hiding place.

You always fill my heart with songs of deliverance.

Whenever I am afraid, I will trust in You.

Let the weak say "I am strong in the strength of the Lord."

I will trust in You.

Selah/Hiding Place: You Are My Hiding Place

6. Can hard things be good?

(To God I wondered...)

What if Your blessings come through raindrops?

What if Your healing comes through tears?

What if a thousand sleepless nights are what it takes to know You're near?

What if the trials of this life are Your mercies in disguise?

Laura Story/Blessings: Blessings

7. How did God reassure you?

I won't give you more

More than you can take

And I might let you bend

But I won't let you break

And no, I'll never let you go.

Group 1 Crew/Fearless:He Said

8. What did God say to you when you were rehearsing all your brokenness?

You are more than the choices that you've made.

You are more than the sum of your past mistakes.

You are more than the problems you create.

You've been remade.

Tenth Ave North/ITunes Session: You Are More

9. What did you say to God when you realized He's never stopped loving you?

But You love me anyway.

It's like nothing in life that I've ever known.

Yes, You love me anyway.

Oh, how You love me?

Sidewalk Prophets/These Simple Truths :You Love Me Anyway

10. Where is God in all of this?

As the thunder rolls I barely hear You whisper through the rain,

"I am with you."

Casting Crowns/Lifesong: Praise You In This Storm

11. You have weathered a few storms. What have you learned? How do you weather the storms of life?

(I say to God)

I'll praise You in this storm

And I will lift my hands,

For You are Who You are

No matter where I am.

Every tear I've cried

You hold in Your hand.

You never left my side

And though my heart is torn,

I will praise You in this storm.

Casting Crowns/Lifesong: Praise You In This Storm

12. How did you know you were in Good Hands?

(I keep hearing Him say...)

I AM holding on to you

I AM holding on to you

In the middle of the storm

I AM holding on to you

Crowder/Neon Steeple: I Am

13. What would you say to God if this cancer doesn't go away?

Even if the healing doesn't come

And life falls apart and dreams are still undone,

You are God

You are good

Forever faithful One

Even if the healing

Even if the healing doesn't come

You are still the Great and Mighty One

We trust you always

You're working all things for our good.

We will sing Your praises.

Kutless/Believer: Even If

14. Cancer treatments can be rough. How did you get through it?

No matter how bad it gets,

I'll be alright...there's hope in front of me!

Danny Gokey/Hope In Front Of Me: Hope In Front Of Me

15. What did you say to God when you realized He had given you Peace in the storm?

Whatever You're doing inside of me

It feels like chaos, but now I can see

This is something bigger than me

Larger than life, something heavenly.

Sanctus Real/We Need Each Other: Whatever You're Doing

16. Why did God give you a second chance?

(I say to God)

You raise me up so I can stand on mountains

You raise me up to walk on stormy seas

I am strong when I am on Your shoulders

You raise me up to more than I can be

Selah/Hiding Place: You Raise Me Up

17. How did you feel when the doctors told you that the Multiple Myeloma was in remission?

Oh, Happy Day

Happy Day

I'll never be the same!

Life Center Worship/This Is Love: Happy Day

18. Where did you say God was in all of this?

Every moment of my life God,

You never left my side.

Every valley, every storm

You were there,

You were there.

Moriah Peters/Brave: You Carry Me

19. Do you have any questions for your readers?

Anybody here found joy in the middle of sorrow,

Peace in the storm,

Hope for tomorrow

And seen it time and time again. Then just say

Amen!

Finding Favor/Say Amen: Say Amen

20. As a survivor, is there anything else you need?

You are all that we'll ever need.

Will Reagan and United Pursuit /Endless Years: Commission

21. Some would say you have been in the grips of an enemy. How did you get free?

Breakin down strongholds of the enemy.

By the blood of the Lamb

Will Reagan and United Pursuit /Endless Years: Commission

22. What happens when strongholds are broken?

...the gates of hell

Will not prevail

For the power of God

Has torn the veil

Now we know Your Love
Will never fail

News Boys/Restart: We Believe

23. What would you say to someone who is ready to give up?

Stay in the fight 'til the final round
You're not going under 'cause God is holding you right
now.

Mandisa/Overcomer: Overcomer

24. Do you have any other advice you'd like to give?

You might be down for a moment,
Feeling like it's hopeless,
That's when He reminds you
That you're an Overcomer

Mandisa/Overcomer: Overcomer

25. Can you trust God's goodness for another?

Whatever it is you may be going through,
I know He's not gonna let it get the best of you.

Mandisa/Overcomer: Overcomer

26. What is God saying to you now that you are feeling better?

I came to give you life!
So spread your wings and fly!
I've got a secret to share!
You're enough to change the atmosphere.
So go and do life BIG!

Jamie Grace/Ready to Fly: Do Life Big

27. You talk about sharing *"His-story"*. How can you do that?

Author of my hope

Maker of the Stars

Let me be Your work of art

Won't You write Your story on my heart?

Francesca Ballestelli/If We're Honest: Write Your Story

28. Are you concerned about the future?

I don't need to know what's next.

You'll be with me every step.

Through it all, through it all

I can see

You carry me!

Moriah Peters/Brave: You Carry Me

29. Can you summarize your faith?

We believe in God the Father

We believe in Jesus Christ

We believe in the Holy Spirit and

He's given us new life

We believe in the Crucifixion

We believe that He conquered death

We believe in the resurrection and He's coming back again

News Boys/Restart: We Believe

30. You are writing a book. Are there any limits to what you would say?

Let my words be life

Let my words be truth

I don't want to say a word unless it points the world

back to You.

I want to be Your Life

I want to be Your Voice

Hawk Nelson/Made: Words

31. Are you writing this for attention?

I don't need my name in lights

I'm famous in my Father's Eyes

Make no mistake

He knows my name

I'm not living for applause

I'm already adored

It's all His stage

He knows my name

He knows my name

Francesca Ballestelli/If We're Honest: He Knows My Name

32. What will you say when this story is finally in print?

I tried to cover my shine

I've tried stayin

In the lines

I, I, I don't wanna hide.

Ready or not here, here I come

I'm about to show you where the light comes from.

Britt Nicole/Gold: Ready or Not

*He put a new song in my mouth, a song of praise to our God; Many will see and fear and put their trust in the Lord (PSALMS 40:3 NASB).

Nuggets

I am a treasure hunter on a *medical journey marathon* remembering and being thankful. You have come into my *His-story* and journeyed with me. Here are nuggets found along the way. They are hidden in your life as well. They might look a little different. Will you find them?

*The bells on my phone still ring seven times a day, reminding me to be thankful and drink water.

*Recalling the directive...Keep telling the Story so God gets the Glory - it's *His-story*.

*Stomping on MM, keeping it under my feet and out of my focus so I can keep my eyes looking up and out. There are things to do, places to go, life to live, and people to love.

*My feet are on the Solid Rock of Jesus, after He lifted me out of a muddy pit...and He's prayed for me!

*I may be in a fiery furnace, but I'm not alone, and there's no smoke on me! (I have my hair and my digestive system is working just fine - now!!!) They will examine me and be amazed and give glory to my God. I will not bow down to this *dis-ease*.

*There is a *Diamond Girl* on the inside...and nothing can touch the *Diamond Girl*. And when God looks at me, it's the *Diamond Girl* that He sees. He is pleased.

*There is also a *Glass Girl* on the inside. If I give all my broken pieces to God, He truly can make something beautiful out of them. I am a work in process.

*The *Outside Girl* may be falling apart, but there is a lot of life left to live.

*The *pits* in life are hard, but there is always a *Hand* ready to lift me out.

*This is like walking on a secret path of uncharted territory, trusting that God has the map and is guiding The Way.

*There really are treasures in the storms.

*Life lessons from the White Water Rafting/Grand Canyon trip. When the water starts to get *poppy* just before the rapids, it's time to hold on with both hands and *suck rubber*. Lean over so the water will go over my head and not hit me full force, or carry me off on the way back out.

*Emotional roller coasters are part of the ride. I can close my eyes and wait for it to be over OR trust that I'm strapped in tight and at least open my eyes, maybe even raise my hands!

*Storm clouds come and just when it's getting really black, somewhere there is a silver lining, a sun beam or maybe even a rainbow...maybe a double.

*I know God is with me; He loves me and has good things planned for me. He has numbered my days and I am ok with what He decides.

*I will continue to pray for healing, and leave the outcome of what that looks like in His hands.

*God is the Great Physician and I remain in His care. He has placed me in a great team of people.

*I have the hope of heaven and a great *family reunion*. My prayer is for all of my family to be there. What a celebration that will be!

*I may need to take naps and slow down. But in doing so, I am finding spectacular things.

*To Be Still and Know He is God takes on a whole new dimension when He brings a swarm of 8,000-10,000 honeybees to our tree for 48 hours. I would have missed it in my 5th gear lifestyle of earlier days.

*Sitting on the deck as the sun goes down being immersed in the spectrum of colors that are growing back from the *hair cut* I gave the hanging flower pots and the overhead colors that dance in the sky: yellow, orange, sky-blue pink, twilight...breath taking.

*And on another night, sitting under a canopy of trumpet vines listening to the hummingbirds get their evening snack and enjoying the sweet company of family.

*Eating fresh peaches right out of the orchard and then finding a bounty of fresh veggies in our yard: *summer goodnesses!*

*Sometimes looking at life through an aquarium is fine! (And necessary!!!)

*Some things need to break before they can be made whole.

*My parent's divorce wasn't my fault.

*There may need to be nudges to get me into a place I need to be.

* Validation is important.

*Taking advantage of *living-life opportunities.* Like roasting marshmallows and enjoying gooey S'mores, boat rides to catch fish and sharing the bounty, sipping tea, catching up with friends and celebrating their life.

*Life lessons from the Stand Up Paddle: keep balanced and if you fall, fall. Just get back up and go again.

* The Great Counselor Who knows everything about me and knows exactly what I need. I really am in Good Hands.

*Don't give God or my husband just a "pizza my heart." Give the whole thing!

*One day I'll trade it all in for an eternity in Paradise without storm warnings.

* I'm just passing through!

*Good-morning texts, sharing meals, cards, prayers, messages, new projects and the pieces to work it out, puppy kisses, chats, rides, lemonade from lemons that are thrown our way, zip-line adventures, neighbor connections, visits and calls from out-of-state family, calls, unspoken thoughts and prayers, stomping team!!!

*Keep watching!

Thanks for listening to my *His-story*.
Farewell.

Bibliography

SCRIPTURES TAKEN FROM HOLY BIBLE:

1. Life Application Study Bible (NIV). New International Version. Wheaton: Tyndale House and Zondervan Publishing, 1988, 1989, 1990, 1991.
2. New American Standard Bible (NASB). Reference Edition. Philadelphia and New York: A.J. Holman Company, 1973.
3. Peterson, Eugene H. The Message (MSG). Numbered Edition. Vol. 2.0. Colorado Springs: NavPress, 2005.

BOOKS:

4. Eggerich, Dr. Emmerson. Love and Respect. Thomas Nelson, 2005.
5. Ferrel, Bill & Pam. Men Are Like Waffles Women Are Like Spaghetti. Eugene: Harvest House Publishers, 2001.
6. Finding Favor. "Say Amen." Say Amen. Prod. Universal Music. 2014.
7. Matheson, George and Mrs. Charles Cowman. Streams in the Desert. Grand Rapids: Zondervan Publishing House/Barbour Publishing, 1928, 1965.
8. Nee, Watchman. Sit, Walk and Stand. Fort Washington: Christian Literature Crusade, 1968.
9. O, Dr. Paul. You Can't Make Me Angry. Capizon Publishing, 2003.
10. Russell, A.J. God Calling. Barbour Publishing, Inc., 1989.

SONGS:

11. Ballestelli, Francesca. "He Knows My Name." If We're Honest. Prod. Word Label Group. 2014.
12. Ballestelli, Francesca. "Write Your Story." If We're Honest. Prod. Word Label Group. 2014.
13. Crowder. "I Am." Neon Steeple. Prod. Six Steps Records. 2014.
14. Crowns, Casting. "Praise You In This Storm." Lifesong. Prod. Reunion Records. 2003.

15. Crowns, Casting. "Voice Of Truth." <u>Lifesong</u>. Prod. Reunion Records. 2003.
16. Finding Favor. "Say Amen." <u>Say Amen</u>. Prod. Universal Music. 2014.
17. Gokey, Danny. "Hope In Front Of Me." <u>Hope In Front Of Me</u>. Prod. BMG Recording. 2013.
18. Grace, Jamie. "Do Life Big." <u>Ready To Fly</u>. Prod. Gotee Records. 2014.
19. Group 1 Crew. "He Said." <u>Fearless</u>. Prod. Fervent Records. 2012.
20. Hawk Nelson. "Words." <u>Made</u>. Prod. Fair Trade Services. 2013.
21. Kutless. "Even If." <u>Believer</u>. Prod. Tooth & Nail Records. 2012.
22. Life Center Worship. "Happy Day." <u>This Is Love</u>. Prod. Life Center Worship. 2010.
23. Littrell, Brian. "In Christ Alone." <u>In Christ Alone</u>. Prod. Reunion Records. 2005.
24. Maher, Matt. "Lord I Need You." <u>All The People Said Amen</u>. Prod. Thank You Music. 2013.
25. Mandissa. "Overcomer." <u>Overcomer</u>. Prod. Captial Records. 2013.
26. News Boys. "We Believe." <u>Restart</u>. Prod. Fair Trade Services. 2013.
27. Nicole, Britt. "Ready Or Not." <u>Gold</u>. Prod. Capital Records. 2012.
28. Peters, Moriah. "You Carry Me." <u>Brave</u>. Prod. Brickhouse Entertainment. 2014.
29. Sanctus Real. "Whatever You're Doing." <u>We Need Each Other</u>. Prod. Sparrow Records. 2008.
30. Sanctus Real. "Whatever You're Doing." <u>We Need Each Other</u>. Prod. Sparrow Records. 2008.
31. Selah. "You Are My Hiding Place." <u>Hiding Place</u>. Prod. Curb Records. 2004.
32. Selah. "You Raise Me Up." <u>Hiding Place</u>. Prod. Curb Records. 2004.
33. Sidewalk Prophets. "You Love Me Anyway." Prod. Word Label. 2009.
34. Story, Laura. "Blessings." <u>Blessings</u>. Prod. Fair Trade Services. 2011.
35. Tenth Ave North. "You Are More." <u>Light Meets The Dark</u>. Prod. Provident Label Group. 2010.
36. Will Reagan and United Pursuit. "Commission." <u>Endless Years</u>. Prod. United Pursuit Records. 2012.

Made in the USA
Charleston, SC
28 April 2016